BATTLE
FOR YOUR
SOUL

BATTLE
FOR YOUR
SOUL

EXPOSING THE PLANS OF DARKNESS

WENDY SADD

XULON ELITE

Xulon Press Elite
555 Winderley Pl, Suite 225
Maitland, FL 32751
407.339.4217
www.xulonpress.com

Paperback ISBN-13: 978-1-66289-034-5
Ebook ISBN-13: 978-1-66289-035-2

DEDICATION

To every lost and wandering soul hungry for a move of God, may the Spirit of Truth rest upon you as you read this book. May it ignite a zeal for the Lord that cannot be extinguished. May you find a church community that worships both in Spirit and Truth. May you have greater wisdom and discernment to recognize darkness veiled as light. May you take your place in the Lord's end-time army, fully equipped to battle in a war that has already been won.

ACKNOWLEDGMENTS

Most importantly, I want to acknowledge Jesus, my Lord and Savior. Thank you for your relentless pursuit to save me from the grips of evil. Thank you for leaving the ninety-nine to save me from what you have coined the "Church to Cauldron Pipeline." Thank you for restoring everything the enemy has stolen and catapulting me into Your perfect will. I will honor and praise You all the days of my life.

Apostle Tomi Arayomi, although we have never formally met, if it were not for you and RIG USA, I would never have developed a blazing fire for the Lord and a deep relationship with Christ. You are a pivotal part of my testimony. You saved my life first by returning me to the arms of our Savior. And then, God used you to save my physical life through a miraculous healing at the first Occupy Conference at RIG Global Church. I am forever grateful. If it were not for you, this book would've never been written.

Thank you, Minister Alivia Blackson-Orr. Your spiritual discipleship and wisdom have been paramount to my growth in Christ. Thank you for your guidance as I have navigated the refining fire of the Lord and as I grow in the prophetic gifting upon my life.

Mom, I love you. Thank you for the years of prayers that sustained me in the wilderness and that helped lead me home. You carry the voice of the Lord, and I value the discernment you carry.

To my three wild and wonderful boys Logan, Blake, and Vance. Your energy is inspiring. I am so grateful for your patience and perseverance through life's challenges. I thank God for each of you and pray your relationship with the Lord grows stronger daily. I pray you walk out these truths, become mighty spiritual warriors to advance the Kingdom of God, walk out your purpose with boldness and integrity, and win souls for the Kingdom of Heaven.

TABLE OF CONTENTS

The Awakening

ALL WITCHES, WIZARDS, and warlocks understand what I am going to tell you. All Satanists and Luciferians understand what I am about to tell you. Some God-fearing, churchgoing people know the information I am about to reveal to you...but many refuse to believe, discuss, or even act upon it.

I can assure you that no one told me the truth in its entirety. As a teenager, I had to figure it out for myself in the darkness of a movie theater.

Maybe people are afraid of what might happen to them, which is why they don't discuss it. Instead, they engage in a game of "ignorance is bliss." There is more peace of mind in ignorance than in being aware of the truth and accepting responsibility for it.

Those who have heard about what is happening in the realm of the spirit may be concerned about their kids learning the truth. If they choose to inform their children, it's usually one-sided, with an emphasis on the happily ever after, and an omission of the awareness of the darker side. This is positioning many children, teenagers, and young adults to be snared by darkness.

If I tell you, are you mentally prepared enough to hear the truth? Will you choose to fight from a position of victory? Will you be strong enough to face opposition? Will you accept the challenges placed before you? Will you lay hold of the strategies provided to you to defeat the enemy? And will you be brave enough to tell others?

Not too long ago, I decided to tell my kids the truth with no omissions. This isn't little league baseball, where everyone gets a trophy. I am talking about the major leagues, the World Series. Anyone in sports knows you must study your opponent to win the long game. Even the military uses this tactic. You must recognize the enemy, how they move, respond, and react. You need to know the enemy's strategies and tactics and have your plan well-rehearsed.

Knowledge is power. Those who understand their opponent have the greatest chance of standing in victory.

For this reason, I will reveal what every witch, wizard, and warlock knows and what many churches refuse to talk about. I am telling you because we are reaching the end game, and if you haven't already, you will get pulled onto the field. You need to know the truth to defeat the opponent and bring home the win.

Knowledge will equip you with the information necessary to make sound decisions. Your opponent will not be able to deceive you or back you into a corner. Most importantly, those "in the know" can train others to win.

I believe you realize that I am not referring to a baseball game. This is crucial, and it's far greater than you might think. I am as serious as a heart attack when I tell you it is a matter of life or death. There are a few things I need to explain. A few stories that will help you understand the magnitude of what I am about to reveal.

It all started when I was sixteen years old. I was watching a movie with some friends one night. It was an end-of-the-world, doomsday apocalyptic film. I'd call it a B film with a modest budget, but that would be too kind. It was awful.

It was one of those movies that was painful to watch. It had a depressing and scary plot, and the actors read their scripts. Word. For. Word. The movie hurt to watch and it felt like it would continue until the end of the world did strike.

My thoughts drifted as I sat there painfully witnessing the world burn to the ground. I was wondering about my upcoming track meet, who I would be competing against, how I should prepare, and whether or not the attractive Spanish exchange student would be present. It made for a much better story.

However, as I sat there, something strange happened. It was a first. One minute, I was buried in my thoughts; the next instant, I heard a voice speaking to me. It wasn't a loud, bellowing voice from the outside but rather a quiet internal voice that sounded much like mine. The voice communicated clearly and left no room for interpretation. It interrupted my inner dialog about the track meet and told me two things about my future.

My thoughts raced with questions about where the voice came from. "Am I just hearing things?" I wondered. No. I obviously heard an internal voice and comprehended what it said. It terrified me so greatly that I began looking around, hoping it had come from somewhere else.

Had I heard an actor in the movie? There is no way. They were too preoccupied with avoiding asteroids, fallen angels, and nuclear bombs.

Was it one of my friends? Nope. The majority of them were sleeping. Was it someone behind me? Yes. That had to be it. Someone was there. I quickly turned around to catch the person sitting behind me. There was not a single person. All I could see was row after row of empty seats. I sat there stunned and in disbelief. This was the first time I heard words in my mind that were not generated from my thoughts.

As a child, I often encountered supernatural events that made me self-conscious, and wondered if other people had these same experiences. I wanted to know what was happening, and, in those moments, I desperately wished I had someone to talk to about it.

I often had dreams that would come true, I knew things about other people I should have never known, and I had several scary encounters at night with a creature that lived under my bed. And yes, it was all real. However, I had never heard words in my voice that were not generated from my mind; this was a first. As the shock of hearing a voice out of thin air wore off, I no longer cared where the voice came from. My attention turned toward what the voice had said.

Could what I had just heard be true? Was it important? Why did I need to know this information now if it was about my future, especially when I was strategizing my "accidental" run-in with the good-looking foreign exchange student during the track meet? Couldn't this have waited for another twenty years?

How would you feel? You are sixteen. You are sitting in a theater, minding your own business, and suddenly, you hear words in your head, in your voice, yet words that did not originate from your mind. The words reveal a prophecy of two things to come. The voice says, "You will become spiritual at the age of forty-two, and you will live through revelations."

Seriously, I can't make this stuff up! I quickly turned around, still thinking someone was playing a joke. No one was there. I listened for more details, but the voice disappeared. I wanted desperately to know more. Mainly, "What does this message even mean? Why are you telling me this now? I am only sixteen."

I never told anyone what happened that day. Even if I had, who would believe me? The last thing I wanted was to end up in a straitjacket and tied to a hospital bed. So, I kept it a secret. It was a secret that tormented me for thirty years. I had no one to talk to who would understand, and I was left to interpret and shepherd the message on my own.

I had thought about telling someone at our church, but no one there ever spoke about the spirit realm. The church was bound by logic and reason. If it didn't occur within the realm of the five physical senses, it was demonic, a topic they avoided at all costs, even at the detriment of their youth having encounters such as these.

I therefore had to solve this riddle on my own without the assistance of an experienced friend or mentor. I thought about this message in solitude for many years to follow. What did it all mean? Why was I told at a young age?

At eighteen, I had figured out what the prophecy had meant. My interpretation went something like this, "It's party time! If I am going to become spiritual at age forty-two, I don't have to worry about religion or God right now. I am going to live until at least the age of forty-two! That's what the voice said. That means I am invincible!"

I believed I could do whatever I wanted and would not die.

Can you see where this is headed? The lack of sound spiritual discipleship led me to believe the prophecy was true and to interpret it on my own, which led me down a terrifying path of destruction.

Without a doubt, I knew the second half of the prophecy meant I would live through the end times, which wouldn't occur until after I turned forty-two. This understanding created a stir in me like no other. I was determined to test this interpretation of the prophecy at every turn in my life. I lived without any regard for God until the age of forty-two.

For twenty-eight years, I lived like every day was my last. I lived on the edge; I enjoyed extreme sports, tattoos, fornication, adultery, idol worship, drugs, alcohol, witchcraft, and pulling my friends down with me. In high school, I graduated with the senior superlative of "The Biggest Dare Devil." In college, I joined a sorority and two years later, I got kicked out that sorority for unruly conduct. There was no stopping me.

I had an abortion. I had children. I got divorced. I had no remorse. You name it, I did it. I lived a reckless lifestyle throughout adulthood, believing I was invincible; then, I turned forty-two.

It was like clockwork. The prophecy came to pass like Cinderella leaving the ball at midnight. Like that, the cyclone of destruction I had been riding stood still, dropping me smack into reality. I landed hard, and I needed God immediately.

So, I set out to seek encounters with God. I needed to experience his presence. I needed to talk to him. I needed to apologize. I needed to know He forgave me. I needed to make things right as a scary revelation woke me from my slumber. I saw that my worldly existence was a mere illusion. I knew this "Earth School" was but a moment in time compared to the eternity lying beyond once my physical avatar had faded away. I began to understand how my decisions and actions in the physical world affected the spiritual dimension, my future, and the future of my children.

I didn't begin actively seeking God through spiritual encounters until I was forty-two years old. I did this partly because I knew the prophecy's time had come but largely because I sorely needed to make changes in my life.

I needed God; however, I had learned at an early age that I wouldn't find Him in church. So, as I set out on a genuine quest to find Him, I ended up under the tutelage of witches, wizards, and warlocks.

Witches, Wizards, Warlocks, and Warfare

Are you ready to learn the truth? Do you want to know what all witches, wizards (Yes, there are still wizards today.), and warlocks know and what many people refuse to discuss? What I am about to tell you will change your life, and the rest of the pages that fill this book will deliver an understanding that will be used as a weapon against the enemy because knowledge is power.

Who do you believe you are? Think about that question for a few minutes. What answer comes to mind? If you want, put the book down and take a few minutes to think about it.

You are not your flesh and bones. Yes, you have a physical body with a heart that supplies vital nutrients to your organs and a skeleton that supports your movement. However, your physical body is just an avatar.

You also have a soul. Your soul consists of your mind, will (your decisions), and emotions.

However, "you," the real "you," is a spiritual being in physical form. For example, you play as an avatar in most video games today. When you die in the game, you still linger around the game without the physical body. Have you noticed this? It is based on truth. You are a spirit using a physical body to navigate this world, this third dimension.

Every witch, wizard, and warlock knows that our physical bodies are only used to traverse this physical realm, and our spiritual bodies live inside the physical body. To put it plain and simple, you are a spiritual being living an Earthly experience.

Every witch, wizard, and warlock also knows that we are immortal. Your spirit lives beyond death. When we die, we leave our physical body and continue to exist spiritually.

Where do we go within the spiritual realm when we die? That is a great question. There are two places for spirits to dwell after a physical death. We either go to Heaven or Hell. (Going to Hell, however, is called the second death.)

Seriously, think about that. You will spend eternity in one of those two places; either Heaven or Hell. Your time in Earth School is a blink of an eye compared to the eternity you will spend in one of those two places. I once heard someone explain how long eternity lasts. They compared eternity to grains of sand in the desert. He said each grain of sand is like 1000 years. Imagine picking up one grain of sand every thousand years until the desert was empty. Eternity has no end and no beginning; it knows no time. Your spirit will go to one of two places when you die, Heaven or Hell; and it is there where you will spend eternity.

How do you know if you will go to Heaven or Hell? The answer depends on your decisions while attending "Earth School." You were created with free will, which means you make choices in life. You have the freedom to be kind or mean to others, use clean speech or profanity, be life-giving or life-taking, say no to drugs and alcohol, abstain from premarital sex or live a sexually immoral life, forgive or condemn others, among many other choices. You get the point. Every day, we make decisions that will affect our physical future on Earth and our spiritual destination beyond life on Earth.

However, there is one major decision that you will have to make, and it is the game changer. It is so important that I dedicate an entire chapter to address that decision after I reveal a few more secrets of witches, wizards, and warlocks. Hold onto your seats because it's about to get crazy.

Hopefully, you are gaining a deeper understanding of the serious nature of our conversation. We are not talking about baseball games and trophies, nor are we talking about physical battles between warring nation states. We are talking about a spiritual battle for your soul. This battle over your mind, will, and emotions will ultimately determine where your spirit resides for eternity; in Heaven or a Lake of Fire (Hell).

Witches, wizards, and warlocks know that we are spiritual beings living in a physical body. They also know that a battle is taking place on Earth for souls. This is much like a video game, but it is happening in real time during our existence here on Earth. The teams: God's angel armies vs. a prideful Satan.

God created every spirit. He loves us very much and wants to save every human on Earth to take us to Heaven and live with Him for eternity. However, Satan is jealous of humans because God made us in His image, loves us, and gave those who believe in Jesus greater power than Satan himself (more on this later). Satan is so jealous of humans that he is on a mission to take as many people with him to Hell for eternity as he can. He is trying to steal each person's soul (mind, will, and emotions) to separate us from God.

This is spiritual warfare. War is raging all around us in the spiritual dimension. Many people have no idea this is happening, but witches, wizards, and warlocks know, and so do some of God's people. There are spiritual armies waging war from both sides. On the winning side, you have God, His angels, and His believers on Earth who are winning souls and advancing the Kingdom of God on Earth. On the opposing side, you have Satan, his angels of darkness (demons), and the humans he has deceived into doing his work (like witches, wizards, and warlocks.) However, it is important to note that God created Satan, who used to be an angel in Heaven. God has authority over Satan, so they do not have equal rank in the spirit realm. NO ONE OUTRANKS GOD; therefore there is no comparison between God and Satan.

Some humans can see this battle with their spiritual sight; some can sense or even hear it. I can tell you that this is true for several reasons. First, many ancient texts tell us about this battle, such as the Bible and the Sumerian tablets, to name a few. The entire Bible is about this battle for souls. The Bible may be ancient, but it is more current than the daily news!

I can also tell you this battle is real because I have seen it occur. I have witnessed spiritual battles in homes, stores, schools, playgrounds, office buildings, restaurants, churches, government buildings, and concerts, among many other places. These battles occur moment by moment worldwide in the realm of the spirit.

I have seen some of the demons waging these battles. I have seen some that look like green, ghoulish children (seriously). I have seen angels of darkness camouflaged as radiant angels of light. I have seen dark shadowy figures leaning on people as they walk down the street, all hunched over. Once, I even saw hundreds of evil spiritual spiders run off a woman as she walked through a flea market buying old painted pictures. And most recently, I have seen demons that shapeshift within people who don't even know what is controlling them.

I have also seen God's heavenly hosts. One time, in church, I saw hundreds of beautiful Heavenly angels filing down over the altar, one after another. They kept filing into the church from above, filling every row and empty space. After several minutes, I noticed at least one angel standing beside each person. In some instances, one person had many angels surrounding them. I silently asked God why He had sent His angels and what they were doing. At that very moment, the pastor began having the church release their burdens, sorrows, and worries unto God. People began to cry, release what had been troubling them, and give their worries to God. And just as the angels filed in empty-handed, I saw them leaving with their arms full of the people's burdens and worries. They were carrying baskets full of all the things the Lord was relieving them of. It was so beautiful and a sight I will never forget.

I have seen angels of the Lord on the rooftops of houses, buildings, and businesses. I have seen them walking with people on the streets, sitting in cars, and fighting Satan's militia. I am telling you the spiritual world is more real than the chair you're sitting on.

I often get asked if I get scared seeing evil spirits. The answer is absolutely not. Do you know why? There are two reasons. It isn't scary because those with a relationship with Jesus have more power than Satan himself. God gives His children power and authority over all darkness. It is a spiritual law. Demons quiver and bow down to the mighty name of Jesus. Secondly, God did not give us the spirit of fear but peace, love, and a sound mind (see 2 Tim. 1:7).

This might surprise you; "Fear" is not an emotion. It is an evil spirit commissioned by Satan. God gave us power over Satan and Satan's buddy fear, so we don't need to be afraid of any evil spirits.

There was once a great man of God, Smith Wigglesworth, who told the story of an encounter he had with Satan. He was sound asleep one night and was awakened by Satan standing next to his bed. Smith recounts the story, saying as soon as he saw it was Satan who had woken him up, he said, "Oh, it's just you," and rolled over and fell back asleep.[1] This needs to be our response to Satan and all darkness. We do not give our power over to the spirit of fear.

Let me tell you a quick personal story. Several years ago, I stood in line at a store and noticed a woman checking out before me. Her entire, and I mean entire, shopping cart was filled with makeup. She had hundreds of dollars' worth of eyelashes, eye shadow, cover-up, mascara, lipstick etc. I couldn't believe it! I had never seen such a huge, heaping pile of makeup. Her shopping cart was filled to the top. Although her back was to me, I thought, "This woman must be really ugly to need that much makeup!" However, I'd never seen someone that ugly, so I questioned my hypothesis.

As I watched her unload her cart, I realized she didn't even know how to use the makeup she was buying. It was bizarre. I wondered why she bought so much makeup when she didn't even know how to put it on. And then I realized she was trying to hide something. I just couldn't pinpoint what she was hiding; until she turned to look at me.

As the woman turned her head, our eyes met, and for the very first time, I saw a black beady-eyed demon staring back at me. I had never seen the eyes of a demon manifest in the flesh. They were pure evil, completely black, and beady. It was not the "woman" looking at me. The demon was fully aware that I was watching it, and I could tell it was starting to get nervous because the woman began to fumble with her wallet and seemed hurried to pay. As she walked out of the store, she nervously turned to look at me one last time to see what I would do.

That was not the only time I saw this evil spirit. Several years later, I was going to get a pedicure, and as I was walking into the building, I saw the same evil eyes staring at me from across the street. There was a woman who had just left the nail salon whose eyes I had managed to catch. The eyes were all too familiar, and it, too, watched me as I walked past it. It knew that I had recognized it and knew exactly what was happening. Nervously, it watched my every move to see what I would do.

You see, when you have Jesus in your life and live by His rules and principles, you carry His light; that light exposes and casts out darkness. Every. Single. Time.

From Church To The Occult

LOOKING BACK, IT is easy to understand how I got involved in witchcraft. I will forever contend that the lack of biblically based spiritual guidance and the decision of the church to omit or leave out spirituality from its instruction led me to look outside the church for a move of God.

Without the guidance of spiritual discipleship and a Spirit-led church, the hunger to experience God will lead you straight into the hands of Satan, and believe me, the devil will be there waiting for you. This is how I wound up in the "Church to Cauldron Pipeline," along with many others.

I attended a private Christian school from kindergarten through eighth grade and spent eighteen years attending church every Sunday. I had been baptized in water at the age of thirteen and attended events at the church most Friday evenings throughout my teen years. In all that time, no pastor, teacher, or youth leader ever talked about the spirit realm and the ensuing battle for my soul. Pastors would talk about salvation, loving your neighbor, and the importance of hope, which are all extremely important lessons that needed to be taught. However, I was never taught about the spirit realm, the gifts of the Holy Spirit, my authority as a Christian, dreams and visions, how to discern the voice of God, or what it meant to see in the spirit. Yet many of these things were active in my life as a child. I was so confused as to why my church didn't acknowledge these things were real, why they didn't speak about them, and why I had to be the one experiencing them all alone.

Ever since childhood, I could listen to someone talk and know, without hesitation, if they were lying or telling the truth. I could watch a person or look into their eyes and know what they were thinking but not directly saying. I understood their motives. If they were lying, I knew exactly why they chose to lie and what they hoped to accomplish. Somehow, when it came to other people, I understood the unspoken. I knew things about them I should never have known.

I never felt comfortable around large crowds because I knew exactly what people were feeling, yet not saying. It made me uncomfortable as I felt like I was invading people's privacy. I hated attending church because I could see people living double lives. When they were in church, they pretended to be pious and moral people, yet they would hide their real identities from Monday through Saturday.

I remember as a child, my parents often talked with a well-dressed man after church each Sunday. The man was always dressed in fancy suits, and I mean fancy shiny suits. As my parents spoke to him one day, I remember thinking, "Why are Mom and Dad talking to a man who likes to wear dresses? He is totally creepy. How could they be friends with this guy?" The man was a cross-dresser! And worse yet, I thought my parents knew he wore women's clothing around his house. I came to find out when I was older that they had no idea.

On a different Sunday, I noticed two church elders, a man and his wife, sitting in the front row of the church. To my amazement, I recall wondering, "Why are they acting like they are madly in love when they can't stand one another and were screaming at each other on their way to church?" I knew many people's dirty secrets, and it was very uncomfortable to be around them.

There aren't many people who will express their true feelings. Many people attempt to conceal the truth and speak what they believe others want to hear. I didn't like being in the company of those who did this because I could see the truth in their hearts. As a result, it was tough for me to trust anyone.

This had an impact on my friendships. I never had many friends because I recognized that most people did not speak about what they truly felt and believed. I gravitated toward people who spoke consistently with their hearts. I felt much more comfortable having two or three close friends. And although I had a few friends, I often felt very alone as I had no one to speak to who would understand what I was experiencing.

I had many supernatural experiences as a young child. Yet, I did not learn the truth about spirituality and what lies beyond the realm of the physical five senses until adulthood. It wasn't until I was forty-two that I received confirmation that we live in a reality with multiple dimensions. There are spiritual beings that operate within and move between these dimensions. This is information all witches, wizards, and warlocks are aware of and regularly utilize to manipulate and capture souls for Satan. Sadly, it is information many Christians do not know, choose not to believe, or just choose not to think about it.

I operated in rebellion for twenty-four years based on a voice I heard at age sixteen. It took me a long time to grasp that I was engaged in a genuine war raging for my soul, and I wanted to do everything in my power to make sure I wasn't captured again. I was tired of being a victim of this conflict. I needed to find God as I had made many mistakes in my life, and I had to locate him quickly.

The Enemy realized I was on a quest to find God, repent, and rekindle a long-lost relationship with Him. That is when the Enemy changed his tactic. The evil forces operating against my life shifted their battle plan and imprisoned me once again. This time, the devil came camouflaged as chakras, light language, crystals, and "energy healing."

At forty-two, I was desperately seeking the presence of God and could not find him in the local churches. There were no miracles, signs, or wonders taking place in any of the churches I attended. Everyone left church each Sunday entirely untouched and returned the next week unchanged, if not in a worse physical, mental, and spiritual state. It didn't sit well within my spirit nor make any logical sense. I knew experiencing God had to be life-transforming, and I had to find Him.

During this search, the devil, once again, snared my soul, this time to the "New Age" movement, which is nothing new at all. The kingdom of darkness repackaged and rebranded ancient occult practices, demonic power, and idol worship as energy healing, quantum physics, and "angels of light." These are the same hermetic laws and demonic principalities that witches, wizards, and warlocks have operated under throughout time. Modern culture merely rebranded them as trendy, safe, and effective practices.

Let's face it, most people who are looking for ways to reduce stress would much rather do yoga and partner with an "angel of light" than find the nearest tatted-up warlock with horns and a split tongue to cast a spell in order to bring them peace. Listen, the devil got clever. He rebranded his old schemes with Western culture in mind so the masses would pursue and consume them.

I was deceived. I gobbled up the devil's Wheaties. I bought into the New Age hook, line, and sinker because it was in the presence of my "spiritual mother," Ana, that I began to experience signs, miracles, and wonders. I believed I had finally found God in her presence.

I spent hundreds of hours studying and meditating under her direction and guidance. I engaged with the supernatural world through these experiences to get closer to God because I had never experienced Him in church. I never saw a single miracle in church. No healings. No deliverances or casting out of demons. No prophesying. Nothing. Pastors would talk about God, but I never witnessed or experienced the Holy Spirit. I decided that if I wanted to experience the Holy Spirit, I needed to search elsewhere. And on my quest to experience Him, I met witches and wizards along the way. I know that sounds crazy. How can someone be looking for God and end up meeting witches, wizards, and warlocks?

I will tell you how. Satan is very deceiving, and he cloaks himself as an angel of light, or a "good guy," to deceive those who don't know any better. Satan rarely portrays himself as evil. He wraps many deceitful lies in beauty, so his evil plans appear Heaven-sent, which can make discerning or recognizing Satan's evil so difficult.

I had no idea I had marched into the devil's office the first time I met with Ana. She was kind, very pretty, and mild-mannered. She was very knowledgeable about old-world mystery school secrets and told fantastic stories of her supernatural encounters. She even referenced the Bible.

You see, Ana was considered a "walk-in." A walk-in is a "benevolent spirit" that takes over a person's body during a traumatic event or a near-death experience (NDE). There are not many "walk-ins" in the New Age movement. They are considered quite special people with extraordinary knowledge and abilities. So, when Ana took me under her wing, I felt honored.

Ana was well-known in the New Age movement. She would often get pulled aside by the military-industrial complex's men-in-black (Yes, they are real.), put in an unmarked car, driven to an undisclosed location, and questioned. She was questioned about upcoming events, both global and universal, as she quite literally sat on a council with "intergalactic" beings. The military complex began to work with her so often that they nicknamed her "Ninety-Five" because of her accuracy in predicting the future. They valued her knowledge so much that they gave her a lanyard with access to a

Deep Underground Military Base (D.U.M.B) to seek shelter during times of trouble on the surface of the Earth.

When she took me under her wing, I felt honored. I wanted to learn everything I could about the old-world mystery school secrets and tap into the power she embodied. It was in her presence that I thought I would find God. (Satan is a liar.)

I would frequently hear stories about her walk-in experience while under her tutelage. Ana's current spirit manifested itself in her "physical body" as a toddler. She experienced a traumatic event when she was young, which brought about a near-death experience (NDE). When the young girl's spirit left the body, the spirit known as "Ana" slithered in.

Ana would frequently tell me stories, in great detail, of galactic wars she had personally witnessed before humanity was established on Earth. She would tell these stories with great emotion and specificity, which only someone present during the wars could recount. One day, we got into a discussion about the planet Nibiru and the Anunaki. She insisted Nibiru would not circle back into Earth's atmosphere as it had been struck and broke apart, forming what we know today as the Kipper Belt. How did she know? She was there, and she witnessed it.

She often shared pictures and stories of her travels worldwide to stabilize the energy grid and ley lines across the globe, to open and close specific portals to allow "benevolent" beings to enter the planet to restore the Earth. Spaceships would follow her, and otherworldly beings would present themselves in her photos. Hundreds of dolphins would gather around her while visiting the ocean. Three-foot-tall thunderbirds would manifest in her presence. Even earthquakes and strange weather patterns would occur upon her entrance into certain territories.

These things never sat right with me, and, in my heart, I questioned what was happening in her life. However, I was willing to tolerate strange anomalies to order to learn old-world mysteries and ancient secrets and experience miracles, signs, and wonders.

There were times when God tried to pull me out of the New Age witch-craft I was involved in, but I was too blinded to know it was Him. I could see spiritual entities in the physical realm, yet I could not recognize when the God I loved so much was reaching out to save me. I, unknowingly, had allowed Satan to blind me spiritually.

After several years of practicing New Age witchcraft, the Lord had enough. He started sending me signs and revealing secrets about my spir-itual mother that she did not want me to know.

One day, I sat with Ana, talking about world events, as we often did, and I heard a noise from the window behind me. It diverted my attention from her, and I turned around to uncover the source of the strange sound. I didn't see anything unusual until I turned around to continue talking with her about the potential for a shift in Earth's magnetic fields.

As I turned to look at her, Ana was gone. She was totally gone. I could no longer see her. I could still hear her voice carrying on the conversation as if nothing was happening, but I could not see her. Instead of her eyes, I saw two brown and yellow slits like a serpent's eyes. Instead of a nose, there were holes for nostrils. Instead of a mouth, there was a forked tongue, and instead of smooth skin, there were small greenish-brown scales. Ana was not who she had claimed to be. I saw the real Ana, the spirit operating through Ana. The spirit that entered Ana during the near-death experi-ence she encountered as a child was a reptile in the form of a serpent.

God had revealed the real Ana to me as she had shape-shifted into a reptilian just long enough for me to witness the truth and for her not to realize what had happened. And what did I do? You are not going to believe this... I did absolutely nothing! Most people would have run out of the room. God had revealed to me whom I was speaking with, and I brushed it off like she was having a bad hair day, as if shapeshifting is an everyday occurrence. Come on! The devil had psychologically blinded me, but the Lord was on a rescue mission.

Looking back, I can see instances where God attempted to get my attention by sending red flags or warnings. Each of these red flags caused me to sit up and think about what I was doing. Unfortunately, I was too quick to dismiss them. One such incident was shocking and completely unexpected.

One morning, I woke up at three a.m., quoting what sounded like Bible verses, words I did not know, but God wanted me to hear. I hadn't read the Bible in fifteen years, yet I woke up declaring, "Seek ye to serve God, and He will be the measure of thy strength. Blessed are those who are poor in iniquity." I had no idea what iniquity (generational sin) was and had to look it up to make sense of the words pouring out of my mouth.

I sat awake for a few minutes trying to capture everything I was saying by typing it onto my phone, but I just couldn't keep up. It was coming fast and furious. So, I laid back down and eventually fell asleep for several hours until the Lord woke me again at 5 a.m.

Thankfully, He was relentless. This time, He had given me a vision of a Bible sitting on the shelf at a local outlet store. I could see it clearly in the vision. It was a black hardback Bible with gold lettering on the spine. It sat on the second shelf of a white bookcase located on the right-hand side of the store entrance. It was there waiting for me to buy it, and a ribbon marked the page I was to read.

I immediately planned my workday around going to buy the Bible. I took the first few hours off work and drove to the store. I arrived before the store opened and waited anxiously outside the doors. When the store opened, I walked in, turned the corner, and saw the exact same book-case God had shown me in the vision. On the second shelf sat the black hardback Bible with gold embossing. I took the Bible off the shelf, turned to the page marked with a satin ribbon, and read a verse aloud.

"Look to the Lord and His strength, seek his face always" (see 1 Chron. 16:11). It confirmed the words I had been speaking at 3 a.m. I couldn't believe it. I bought the Bible, brought it home, placed it on my bookshelf, and didn't open it again for another two years. Instead of realizing that this was God's way of communicating with me to change directions, I took it as a sign that I was on the right path. I continued to study with witches and wizards.

I had spent three years, unknowingly, chasing demonic power. The Lord sent me sign after sign to seek His strength and His face. He was telling me this because the one whom I was seeking was not Him. Ana was not of God or His strength but of the devils'. Yet, I was still ignorant and blinded by evil veiled as light.

I am grateful for God's unwavering perseverance. He did not give up on me that day and continued to send me signs. He knew He would have to work through the enemy to save me. The Lord knew I was so entrenched in the occult that He used a psychic reading from Ana to lead me to a real man of God named Apostle Tomi Arayomi, whom God would later use to save my spiritual and physical life.

In the fall of 2021, "Ninety-Five" was reading my "Akashic Records" and telling me about my future for 2022. (The Akashic Records serve as a counterfeit to God's Book of Life, and they are straight from the pits of Hell. They are demonic record books intended to thwart people from their destinies. If you have engaged in the opening of these records, you have shifted the realm of the spirit away from God's purpose for your life and handed your destiny over to the devil. *The Battle For Your Soul* will guide you on how to get your life back in alignment with all that God has for you.) Ana would tell me about each month of the upcoming year and advise me on navigating that time in my life. She told me January 2022 would be a time of "life-changing opportunities." I would not have much time to decide to act on these opportunities, as they would leave as quickly as they presented themselves. She instructed me to take immediate action when these moments arrived. I wouldn't have time to think about them, and if I did not act on them, my life would never be the same.

During that same time, I was watching videos with predictions for the year 2022. As I was searching, a video appeared on my YouTube feed from a Godly man, Apostle Tomi Arayomi titled, "Nine Years Left."[2] God started working on my heart and renewing my mind when I started watching the video. Not only was God reminding me of everything He had been showing me about Ana, but now He had shown me a video of a Godly man who hears directly from Him.

I thought I was on the correct course to find God for years. I had finally witnessed miracles. Miracles I'd never witnessed in church were taking place right in front of my eyes. Learning alongside Ana, I was even seeing wonderous healings, hearing accurate prophesies, and encountering beings of "light." I was sure I had found God. I was positive I had found God… until I saw Apostle Tomi's video.

Thoughts started circling my mind like vultures devouring flesh. It was messy. God was removing old, conditioned mindsets and replacing them with a newfound hope. If you could hear the cacophony in my mind, it would have sounded much like this, "This Apostle Tomi can hear from God? He has spiritual encounters? God uses him to advance His work on Earth. Who is Ana working for? She never speaks of Jesus the way Apostle Tomi does. She does not have a relationship with Jesus like he does. She does not refer to the Bible or reveal biblical understanding as he does. Ana is not working for the God whom I wish to serve? Whoa! Is that why she shapeshifted? Ana works for Satan! Apostle Tomi is working for the *Living*

God I have been searching for. Apostle Tomi has a relationship with Jesus! I want to know God in that way. This is what I have been searching for all these years! Apostle Tomi can show me God. I gotta watch another one of his videos…"

At that moment, I realized Satan had single-handedly stolen my soul. I was losing the battle I was so desperately trying to win. How did this happen? How could I reverse what I had done? What started as a quest for God was a downward spiral toward an eternity in Hell.

In January 2022, I came across a course Apostle Tomi would teach only a few days before the registration. I started wondering if I should register for the class. I grew very worried. How would God forgive me for what I had done and want to use me to tell others about Jesus when I had unknowingly partnered with the devil for thirty-six years? Why would He want a relationship with me? I had broken every rule in the Bible. Why would He ever choose me?

Then, God used what was meant for evil for good! God used the words of a shapeshifting witch to lead me straight to Apostle Tomi's ministry. Unbelievable? Maybe so. But God's ways are not our ways! God reminded me of Ana's directions for January. "Life-changing opportunities will pass you by if you do not seize the moment. Don't think. Just act. Your life will never be the same if you don't take hold of the opportunities."

I registered for the class at that moment, not knowing the magnitude of change that would transpire in my life.

After hearing the man of God, Apostle Tomi, speak on the first day of class, I recommitted my life to Christ and began fasting, praying, and reading the Bible. I made plans to get baptized again by water and spirit and threw away all the New Age clutter and lingering mindsets.

And just like that, The Holy Spirit stepped into my life, and Ana stepped out. I never spoke to her again.

On that first day of class, I threw away over $25,000 of crystals, tarot cards, oracle cards, pendulums, dream catchers, pictures, crystal wands, flower essences, candles, books, feathers, Reiki and other healing course materials and certificates, massage tables, tuning forks, merkabas, sorority insignia/pictures, healing music, lucky rabbits paws, four leaf clovers, dragon claws, healing stones/bracelets, horoscopes, books on telekinesis, hermetic laws, sacred geometry materials, my remote viewing work, potions, sage, charged cotton, etc.

(I often get asked why I didn't sell the items and recoup the money. Honestly, my new life with Christ is priceless. Although it has cost me much more than just money to live with holiness and integrity for Christ, it pales in comparison to the price the Lord paid when He died on the cross for our sins.)

What felt the most satisfying was throwing away my family's 32nd Degree Scottish Rite Freemason ring that had been passed down for generations. I believe my family's involvement in Freemasonry stems back to the Revolutionary War with a wealthy relative who gave George Washington a large sum of money to fund his efforts. This currency exchange gave him direct access to the upper echelons of the secret society. The involvement continued down the family line with a great-great uncle who had given up his 32nd-degree ring on his way to becoming a Master Freemason. I had worn that ring daily for twenty years with great pride, not knowing that the Masonic Order was built on the foundation of occult practices and human sacrifice.[3] It is demonic at its very core, and it is not until members reach the upper echelons (32nd and 33rd degrees) that this secret is revealed.[3] The thought of my relatives knowingly participating in these satanic rituals disgusted me.

Throwing away the ring was symbolic of the power I felt, through the Holy Spirit, to gladly turn my back to the wiles of the devil and make a lifelong commitment to God. I committed to do the work the Lord set out for me, to advocate for the Holy Spirit to operate in the Christian Church and save as many people from the New Age movement as possible. (As I am writing this book, I hear the Lord say, "Wendy, it is time to expose, uproot, and tear down the Church to Cauldron Pipeline.")

Throwing away the ring also represented the deliverance that God's grace would soon bestow upon me. The deliverance I received was not only for myself but also for my entire bloodline, which had been cursed by generations of witchcraft and rebellion.

The Lord pulled me from darkness, thrust me into a season of sanctification (to make holy) and consecration (to make sacred), and began killing my flesh (humanity). In six months, He took my twenty-two-year career in education and crushed my irresponsible spending habit by significantly reducing my income. He cleaned my speech as I no longer cussed, slandered others, or took His name in vain. He destroyed my desire to drink alcohol, watch TV, watch movies, engage in social media, read secular books, and listen to secular music. He removed all witchcraft practices, mindsets, and materials from my home and my life, and He delivered me from demons and demonic oppression over a twelve-month period.

He killed my pride. He took my vanity. And He slaughtered the seducing spirit operating in my life by taking my hair. Yes, quite literally, my hair even fell out without any medical reason; however I know it was spiritual. And as emotionally devastating as this was, I know it was one of the greatest gifts God has ever given me. 1 Corinthians 11:15 states, "*But if a woman have long hair, it is a glory to her: for her hair is given her for a covering.*" God stripped me of my glory to take on His Glory.

He swiftly replaced everything He took away. He gave me a promotion in my career, placing me alongside policymakers in the State Board of Education. He taught me financial stewardship, and healthier eating habits, gave me an insatiable appetite for the Word of God, a stronger and consistent prayer and fasting life, cleared my calendar to give me time to grow spiritually, secured for me a secret place to meet with Him, and He replaced ungodly relationships with new Christ-centered relationships.

God used what was meant for evil for good. He used the words of a shapeshifting witch to lead me to a great man of God who would save my soul from evil disguised as light. God would use Apostle Tomi again several months later to save my physical life from a dangerous growth in my chest through a miraculous healing.

I attended the first Occupy Conference at RIG Global Church in Houston during the Summer of 2022.[4] A month before the conference, I found a growth in my chest that was getting larger, growing tentacles (the best way I could describe it), and was starting to cause pain near my rib cage. By the time I had reached the conference, I could no longer raise my arms in the air because the pain was so great.

One evening, Apostle Tomi said at the conference, "There is someone here with a lump in their chest." And he placed his hand on his body exactly where my growth was. "The fire of God is coming upon you now. The Lord is healing you. The lump is gone. Check it. It's gone. Check it. It's Gone."

As Apostle Tomi is speaking, in my head, I am thinking, "There is no way he is talking about me. There are hundreds of people here. It can't be me." And in that moment, I felt the fire of God for the first time. I was hot and weak, and I felt like I was going to pass out. I could barely stand. As I realized what was happening, I heard the Apostle say again, "Check it. It's Gone. Who are you? Come up here. Who are you?"

I finally got the courage to check my chest. The growth was gone, totally and utterly gone. The growth in my chest, which had grown significantly over several weeks and was both visible and palpable, vanished in seconds in the presence of the Holy Spirit.

I began to walk to the front of the church as Apostle Tomi asked, "Who are you? Come here. Who are you? It's gone." As soon as I made it up to the altar, Apostle Tomi and Dr. Sharon Stone began to pray for me; I collapsed under the power of the Holy Spirit. Later, I watched the video from the conference and heard Apostle Tomi say, "What the devil planned as terminal, God declared temporary." He continued to pray, breaking the generational curse of my bloodline that had started with my mother having cancer in the same spot.

What God did to redirect my life in that short time was nothing short of a miracle. The changes that transpired across a few short months have taken others years to overcome. I am grateful for God's mercy as He realigned my life with His predestined purpose and catapulted me towards destiny. I am more connected to Him and fulfilled than I have been my entire life. Only God can satisfy my soul; I thank God daily, for His mercy, for Rig Global Church, and for Apostle Tomi.

Supernatural Gifts

From childhood, I knew things I should never have known, and I often had dreams that would come true. I did not understand what was happening at the time, but these were supernatural gifts given to me by the Holy Spirit. The Holy Spirit is a Person and He gives spiritual gifts to each human to carry out His work on Earth. He gives them without repentance. That means once He gives you a spiritual gift, you get to keep it, no matter what. It is His gift to you.

There are nine Gifts of the Spirit. You can find them in 1 Corinthians 12:1-11. Which gift(s) did God give you? How can you use them to glorify God and advance the Kingom of God on Earth?

Gifts of Speech
The Gift of Prophesy (To know the future)
Speaking in Tongues (Ability to speak in a Heavenly language)
The Interpretation of Tongues (Ability to understand Heavenly languages)

Gifts of Power
Gift of Faith (Believing in the unseen)
Gift of Healing (Ability to pray for people and they get healed)
Gift of Miracles (Ability to pray and miracles happen)

The Gifts of Knowledge

Words of Wisdom (Using the Words of God to problem solve)

Words of Knowledge (Knowing things you should not know)

Discerning of Spirits (Identifying between the Spirit of God, man, and Satan)

Discernment is key to recognizing your opposition. Discernment means to judge something well or to know the true nature of something.[5] In the case of saving souls, we must be able to discern the work of God from the work of man or Satan. You must be able to see through the camouflage and know that Satan is masquerading as an "angel of light," meaning he appears as doing good when, in reality, his master plan is *to steal, kill, and destroy*" (see John 10:10).

God had gifted me with words of knowledge, the gift of prophecy, and the discerning of spirits; however, my discernment needed strengthening and practice. I say that because although I had that gift, I was still deceived into witchcraft.

Satan designed New Age witchcraft to look harmless and concealed it with beautiful crystals, "Light Language" (demonic tongues), fortune-telling, and miraculous healings. Witchcraft mimics the nine Gifts of the Spirit. What? I'll state it again. Witchcraft can look like the nine Gifts of the Holy Spirit. The gifts God gives us can be used for the Kingdom of God, as they were intended, or they can be used for the Kingdom of Darkness. The only difference is the source or who is the driving force behind them. Who is operating behind your spiritual gifts? Is the Holy Spirit of the Living God driving the gift, or has Satan hijacked your gift?

While studying under Ana, I met other witches and wizards, who thought they were doing good for humanity. Some of them even went to church to worship God! These people genuinely believed they were helping people by reading their fortunes from tarot cards, healing them with potions, realigning their chakras, and performing miraculous spiritual surgeries using crystal wands. They did not realize that Satan had hijacked their gifts and used them to win souls for the kingdom of darkness. The people seeking help from these witches and wizards had unknowingly sold their souls to the devil...regardless of how often they went to church to worship God. This is how good Satan is at tricking people. Many of the New Age witches, wizards, and their clients had fallen prey to the Church to Cauldron Pipeline. Satan tricked all of them.

The witches and wizards I encountered at gatherings, meetings, conferences, and classes during my "training" did not have wart-covered noses. They were not wearing purple robes or pointy shoes, riding brooms, or training dragons. They did not have black, beady eyes like the possessed women I mentioned earlier. They appeared to be typical people who were very friendly and helpful. You wouldn't think anything of them if you saw them on the street. They were dentists, doctors, lawyers, principals, construction workers, teachers, etc., who led "normal" lives. They were very nice people who were seeking to improve their lives and the lives of those they loved.

I learned that they were working with "spirit guides," "angels," and "ascended masters" to do good on Earth. They were healing the sick and helping people acquire wealth, repair broken relationships, and find their "personal" destiny. I watched them manipulate the spiritual realm to manifest or bring about their desires in the physical world. It was here I began to witness many miracles.

They taught me how to do these things out of friendship. Little did I know that I was nowhere near finding God. What had I found? The devil himself disguised as energy healing, quantum physics, and angels of light. The commander of the evil army had separated me from my God. And in my ignorance, I had become a prisoner of war, a victim of the Church to Cauldron Pipeline.

I was looking for God and ended up studying and operating in the world of witchcraft. All of it was veiled in light and science. I was taught that it was "quantum physics." "Harmless" ways to change how I thought and interacted in the metaphysical world to achieve desired results on Earth.

I didn't realize I was interacting with evil spirits concealing themselves as benevolent or kind beings. This was guerrilla warfare at its finest. It wasn't God. I had unknowingly made covenants, or agreements, with evil spirits who would manipulate or change the spiritual realm to affect the physical dimension in which I lived. Total. Witchcraft.

These evil forces can be very difficult to discern. The man responsible for returning my soul to God, Tomi Arayomi, once stated that our battle is not a battle of "good vs. evil" but rather a battle of "good vs. good and evil."[6] The devil mixes good with evil. Something may look good on the outside, but at its core, it has pure evil intent.

I write all this to say, become aware of your spiritual gifts and know, without a shadow of a doubt, that the Holy Spirit is fueling them. Do not fall prey to the Church to Cauldron Pipeline. It is a slippery slope; without discernment or biblically based spiritual discipleship, one wrong step will thrust you into the mouth of the pipeline.

I have spent thirty years wondering who I heard speak to me that night at the movies and why the voice told me about my future. I now understand I had sinful doors open at a young age through my ancestral ties to the Freemasons. However, I had opened another door to Satan one month before I turned sixteen when I lost my virginity. That was the open door that allowed the devil's legal rights to operate in my life, and that is when I started to see things in my life shifting for the worse. It was an evil spirit that spoke to me to throw me off the course that God had ordained for my life. The devil knew I loved Jesus; so he used the open door and the lack of spiritual discipleship to throw me off course. I fell for the bait…hook, line, and sinker and slid right into the pipeline.

Genesis 50:20 states, "*You intended to harm me, but God intended it for good to accomplish what is now being done, the saving of many lives.*" I now understand that God turned my life around for this very moment. It was to set me on a trajectory that would ultimately boomerang me back to him, closer than I could have ever been. It was for this book and a radical testimony to share. Most importantly, it allowed me to warn you about the battle ensuing for your soul, expose the deception of darkness veiled as light, andto give you strategies to combat the enemy and stand in victory through Jesus!

I thank God for protecting me all those years of living in rebellion and contradiction to His word. I thank God for protecting me from seven close calls with death perpetrated by the devil, and I praise His matchless name for bringing me safely back home to His loving embrace.

KNOW YOUR OPPOSITION

I MUST EXPLAIN HOW Satan and his forces operate and their tactics for stealing souls. In battle, it is necessary to study the Enemy. It is just as important to understand the Enemy's strategies and weapons as it is to understand your battle tactics. To stand in victory, you need to be able to predict the Enemy's next move. You must learn to recognize the Enemy no matter how he disguises himself or where he hides. 1 Peter 5:8 explains, *"Your adversary, the devil, walks about like a roaring lion, seeking whom he may devour."*

Heaven is a Kingdom, and God is the supreme ruler, who is seated on the throne. This is why we also call Heaven the Kingdom of God. He is the King over all other kings in existence, The Almighty God. He has power and authority over all of creation.

Kingdoms are governmental systems ruled by a series of laws made by decrees from a king. Once a king makes a decree, it cannot be rescinded or taken back. A king's decree is written on paper, sealed with the symbol on his signet ring, and it remains law until his death.

All creation is governed by physical laws, such as gravity, that God set in place. Every spiritual being is governed under a set of spiritual laws that God has decreed. Every human, angel, demon, and Satan must abide by the same spiritual laws. Even God abides by the spiritual laws He has decreed. The Bible is the legally binding document that outlines all of God's spiritual laws.

Therefore, Heaven and the spirit realm are run like a courtroom. God is sitting on the throne. He is the judge. Jesus sits on the right-hand side of God, and He is the defense attorney for all Christians. Satan is the accuser or the prosecuting attorney, forever going to God and telling Him about our sins (see Revelation 12:10).

There are several ways that Satan can legally steal souls with or without consent. He is given legal access to steal souls through disobedience, covenants, and ignorance, according to Apostle Selman.[7] Believe it or not, this is all a part of a spiritual, legal system bound by spiritual law and written out in the Bible. Unfortunately, Satan is a great accuser and knows these laws better than most men and women. However, knowledge is power, and it is through knowledge that we can win this battle. If we familiarize ourselves with and obey God's rules, Satan cannot accuse us, nor can he receive legal access to manipulate our lives.

However, Satan will stand before God in the courtroom of Heaven and accuse people of sins they have committed. If the person on trial is a Christian and they have repented and turned from the sin, they are acquitted or given a not guilty verdict because Jesus died for the sins of His people. (The blood He shed when He died on the cross justifies Christians' sins. You can think of "justified" as meaning it was "just if I" had never committed that sin.[8]) If the Christian on trial does not repent, Satan is granted legal access to carry out evil plans against that person.

If Satan goes before God to accuse someone who does not believe in Jesus, that person will be guilty as charged, and Satan will be able to carry out legal operations in their life as well. The blood of Jesus will not justify the sin of a nonbeliever. If someone rejects Jesus, they are also rejecting the power of His blood to forgive sins in the courtroom of Heaven. Therefore, they will be guilty on all accounts of their sins.

Many people do not want to know what I am about to tell you. And if they do hear it, they choose not to believe it. This "ignorance is bliss" attitude keeps people in the dark about what is happening around them and through their decisions and actions. As you read, please keep in mind that the purpose of this book is to give you a high-level intelligence briefing on the Enemy's tactics and how to claim your authority to win the battle for your soul. So, let's press onward.

DISOBEDIENCE

God places a hedge, or barrier, of protection around His people. However, disobedience, covenants, and ignorance can cause a breach or break in that hedge. Imagine feeling safe in a home because all the doors and windows are locked. No one can enter the house; no one can reach you. You are completely safe. However, breaking any one of God's laws can open a door or window in that house. All it takes is a small crack to allow Satan's foot in the door to gain access to your life to steal, kill, and destroy.

God knows this, so He is serious about His people following His laws. He does not want Satan to enter your life. Satan comes to steal, kill, and destroy. Jesus came to give life more abundantly (see John 10:10). So, keep that door closed! There is a way to close a door if you open it. We close doors when we repent or ask forgiveness and renounce or turn away from the sin that opened the door. I will go into more detail in a later chapter.

As a child, it was never explained to me that sin opens a door for the devil to manipulate your life. I was told to follow God's laws and commandments because that is what "good people do." What I heard was, "Blah... Blah...Blah..." How many times did I sit through lessons about following rules? I felt smothered with no understanding of why I needed to follow them. I wanted the autonomy to decide for myself and do what I wanted. Getting bossed around gets old very quickly.

I wish someone would have explained what happens in the spirit realm when we do *not* obey God's rules. I would have listened intently and followed His rules had I understood why He put them in place.

Breaking the spiritual laws God has in place has several consequences. First, it is like a soldier going AWOL or running away from duty while on enemy territory. Sinning separates us from God and provides legal grounds for the enemy to imprison us. Satan's evil forces are just waiting for us to leave a door cracked open to steal, kill, and destroy (see John 10:10). God is trying to protect your soul (mind, decisions, and emotions) by ensuring there are no breaches or open doors for Satan to enter your life.

Choosing not to follow God's word has serious ramifications in the spiritual realm. And remember, what happens on Earth must first occur in the spiritual dimension. So, when we sin, we are separated from God. Satan then has legal access to our lives and will set in motion evil plans against us in the spirit realm that could eventually manifest in the physical plane on Earth. It may manifest right away, or it might take years to pass. Regardless of when the evil plan is scheduled to hit, the devil sets the plan in place. I don't mean to sound harsh or try to scare you. I intend to give you the truth and understanding of the importance of following God's laws.

Laws are the work of God. He is, therefore, aware of the consequences of disobeying the law. Satan gains legal access into our lives when we break the law. The effects could become apparent right away or years later. If the door of disobedience remains open, numerous issues may occur. God knows this. Satan knows this, and now you know it too. God is attempting to keep your soul safe. He hopes you will abide by His rules because He wants you protected—bottom line.

I will teach you, later in this book, how to close spiritual breaches that have been opened so you can protect yourself from spiritual attacks. However, one of the first things you must understand are the laws, rules, and regulations that God has set in place and hopes we follow to protect ourselves from ambush. I have listed God's Ten Commandments found in Exodus 20: 1-17 below. These are not the only standards and principles we are called to live by but this is the place to start.

The Ten Commandments from God

You shall…

1. Not have idols other than God
2. Not make idols
3. Not take God's name in vain (Cuss using the name of God or Jesus)
4. Keep the Sabbath Day holy
5. Honor your father and mother (God promises long life to those who do!)
6. Not murder
7. Not commit adultery (Fornicate with another person's wife/husband)
8. Not steal
9. Not bear false witness against your neighbor (Lie about someone, gossip, talk badly, etc.)
10. Not covet (Want something someone else has)

I Samuel 15:23 provides a sobering revelation. The verse states, *"Rebellion is as sinful as witchcraft, and stubbornness as bad as worshiping idols."* Rebellion is a form of disobedience and is held in the same regard as witchcraft, and stubbornness to the Lord is the same as idolatry. Think about your life in terms of rebellion. Have you been rebellious? If so, you have been practicing witchcraft according to the word of God.

As you read this section, consider what has been going well and where you struggle. Where have you left doors open? What are some areas that need your attention and conscious effort? What do you need to ask God's forgiveness to close doors and raise the hedge of protection? What has God asked you to do that you have ignored or put off? You need to repent and do as He has asked.

IGNORANCE

There were once a few acquaintances of mine who claimed they could never obey all of God's rules because there were just too many of them. They don't understand that we are human and God is merciful and forgiving. He knows we are going to make mistakes before they happen. It is human nature to sin. Think about it. You don't have to teach a three-year-old to disobey their parents; they instinctively do so by not listening, throwing tantrums when they don't get what they want, etc. The beautiful thing about God is that He will forgive us as long as we repent and try hard not to repeat the same sin.

I believe my former friends would change their minds if they understood how the spiritual world operates. Some people are not ready for this message because they do not want to change their actions. They just don't want to hear it. This is a form of ignorance, blatant ignorance. Ignorance will be one of the major reasons souls are lost to Satan, and people will spend eternity in Hell. Many God-loving, kind, caring, compassionate people will spend eternity in a lake of fire because of their ignorance and unwillingness to change their ways!

People who do not know or choose not to listen to this truth are handing their souls to the enemy. Yes, they may live a good life in their physical bodies, doing whatever they want with whomever they please, but this existence is a blip on the radar screen. Ignorance will buy them a one-way ticket to Hell for eternity as soon as graduation day from Earth school arrives. God knows this, and that is why he created these rules. He wants us to close all doors to sin so he can secure the hedge of protection around us. He does this so the devil has no legal access to manipulate our lives.

How is it that many practicing witches and warlocks understand the legalities of how sin works, yet so many others are left in the dark? This is what I mean by ignorance. Satan understands the legalities of sin in the realm of the spirit and uses this knowledge to destroy people's lives, yet most people have no idea what is happening. Now that you know the truth, what will you choose to do?

There is more to ignorance than just refusing to hear the truth. There are traps set in place by the Enemy that many do not expect but can have devastating outcomes on a person's life. I will speak to just a few of these below. Since many people just do not know these things or do not think about the ramifications of their actions, I classify these as acts of "ignorance."

Touching/Owning Cursed or Familiar Objects

I was viewing a video with my son a long time ago. The guy in the video bought a truck full of secured antique crates, cartons, and luggage for $10,000. He would pull items out of the boxes individually, hold them up, throw them, smash them with a sledgehammer, or do something ridiculous with the objects. It was quite entertaining. He pulled out some old creepy-looking porcelain dolls, old games, jewelry boxes, a safe, jump ropes, and paintings. Then he pulled out the creepiest-looking trunk. It looked like it came off the set of a horror movie.

He mentioned how creepy the box was and how afraid he was to open it; in fact, he almost didn't. Against his better judgment, his friends eventually talked him into opening the box. The very first object he pulled out was a tribal scepter that looked like it had belonged to a witch doctor. He immediately started feeling sick and couldn't stop talking about how disgusting the scepter was. His friends turned off the video as he instantly fell ill. When they resumed filming, he appeared pale and feeble and remarked, "I wish I had never opened that box."

We can knowingly or unknowingly touch objects that have evil attached to them. Objects can carry a curse or can have evil spirits attached to them. These are called "familiar" objects. There are spirits attached to these objects; if you touch them, bring them home, or wear them, you are opening yourself to attacks from the enemy and demonic activity. In the instance of the video I referenced, he knew something was not right. He was able to discern it. He knew even before opening the box. Yet he opened it anyway. Although he felt better after some time, if the box or items in that box were cursed or had spirits attached to them, he could be in store for more trouble in the future.

Have you ever read about the story of the curse on King Tut's Tomb?[9] It is a classic example of cursed objects. When explorers first entered King Tut's tomb, they noticed an inscription above the entrance that they omitted to follow. It was an omen, or warning, to those who entered and moved the relics. It read, "Death shall come on swift wings to him who disturbs the peace of the King."[9] Shortly after the tomb's opening and removal of its antiquities, people started dropping like flies. A few of these mysterious deaths included the financer of the expedition, who died from a mosquito bite on his face that gave him blood poisoning. The radiologist who took x-rays of the Pharaoh's mummified body died three days later. And even the pilot who moved the relics out of Egypt died shortly after the plane ride. These are just a few people affected by the evil placed over King

Tut's treasures. There were many more. The lesson is that evil can attach itself to objects, so be careful what you choose to touch, purchase, and wear.

Wearing items with symbols of witchcraft or pagan symbols, such as a pentagram, the "Eye of Horus," Egyptian Ankh, etc, can open a door. So can wearing items made with the intent to harm by those who practice witchcraft, knowingly or unknowingly. For instance, I used to purchase jewelry at New Age conventions. Purchasing bracelets crafted from various stones, I would wear them according to my desired method of manipulating the material world. To materialize money, for example, I used to wear carnelian stones. A black tourmaline stone would help me "clear negativity." Not only was this witchcraft because I was using objects to manipulate the real world, but I also didn't know who produced the bracelets or whether it was their intention for me to open a larger door with each use.

Walking on Cursed Land

In Texas, there was a concert in the summer of 2021. Social media was ablaze with reports of numerous concertgoers falling ill, and authorities were baffled as to why.[10] Later in the show, people lost their minds as fans became enraged and trampled on one another in a panicked frenzy. There were many injuries and several deaths during that concert.[10] I can guarantee it was orchestrated and organized in the spirit realm before the concert date. I would even guess that a covenant, or agreement, was made between the music artist and Satan before the event, a trade of sorts, human sacrifices for wealth and influence.

Demons can manipulate humans by either possessing them or oppressing and controlling them from the outside. Fans inadvertently attended a concert where a pact with the devil was made. Fans did not explicitly consent for this to happen to them; nevertheless, by attending the show, they gave both physical and spiritual approval for it to happen.

They came into agreement with this attack by paying for the ticket and entering the concert. Unknowingly, that was their "yes." Ignorance opened the door, allowing the enemy to infiltrate and ensure devastating consequences. Unfortunately, there are probably attendees of that concert who still have evil operating in their lives that they cannot shake. I pray for their deliverance, spiritual wisdom, and repentance.

There have been concerts within the last year with demonic rituals conducted on stage, and attendees have gotten "amnesia" or forgotten parts of the show.[11] The media will say it was "over-excitement." I will contend that it was a demonic spell by way of the rituals the attendees unknowingly agreed with, merely by being present at the concert. The Lord does not want this for his people. He wants us to be at the right place at the right time!

The Wickerman Man Festival is another example of people making covenants due to walking on cursed land. You had better sit down because this will surprise you. Let me explain the history behind the festival before I show you how the devil got creative and hid pure evil intent behind peace, love, and the beauty of nature.

The Wickerman Festival was an ancient Pagan Celtic Festival run by Celtic Pagan Priests.[12] They would build a gigantic effigy or human-like structure, from sticks and pieces of highly flammable dry wood. They would fill these "wickerman" statues with people and animals. Yes, they were living people and animals! Sometimes, the people would be prisoners of war or criminals, but they would kidnap and place other people in the effigy if they did not have access to them. At the end of the festival, the Pagan Priests would light the wickerman, filled with people and animals, on fire as living sacrifices to please their angry gods. They would use this ritual in times of plagues, war, famine, and other times of distress in hopes that their gods would help them.

Can we agree that this is entirely demonic? Now, fast-forward hundreds of years…

A similar festival occurs in the Deserts of Nevada every year. Attendees at the festival claim that the festival's purpose is to promote a sense of community, acceptance, nature, and self-expression through creative powers.[13] Sounds beautiful. Right?

However, many people engage in occult practices and satanic rituals during the festival. At the end of the festival, a giant wooden human effigy, or human-like structure, is lit on fire. Although they are not burning people and animals alive anymore, this is still an occult Pagan practice symbolizing the burning or destruction of man, who was made in God's image. Now, can you see how the devil can mix something that sounds good with evil?

Many of those who attended the festival were engaging in ungodly acts that were also occurring during the days of Noah. And at the 2023 Burning Man Festival in Black Rock, God flooded the desert. It rained hard for days! Thousands of people were stranded in the desert, unable to move their vehicles, in or out of the desert, due to the thick, wet mud that was acidic and burning people's skin. People were stranded for days without food, supplies, toilets, and clean, dry clothes.[13]

Although they got off easy on this one, attending this festival has opened a door for evil to operate in the attendee's lives. When Satan stands before God to accuse them of witchcraft and idolatry (at the least), if they deny Jesus and have not repented, Satan will be granted legal access to interfere in their lives. It's how the courtroom of Heaven works.

Going to this festival is deceiving. It sounds harmless. However, the spiritual ramifications of attending may have very detrimental effects on those who attended. Just by being at the festival, they have come into agreement, or covenant, with witchcraft, which will bring about bloodline curses.

Please be aware of where you go and what you may be coming into agreement with, knowingly or unknowingly, by resting your feet on that ground, whether it be a concert, festival, home, vacation, etc. Always keep your eyes peeled for signs that you may be opening a spiritual door that God wants you to keep closed.

BLOODLINE OR GENERATIONAL CURSES

It is essential to mention that many people are under bloodline or "generational" curses and do not realize it. Yes, Christians, too! Many people think that they are free from demonic attacks because they have accepted Jesus as their Savior. In reality, Christians are way more prone to these attacks, as the devil's purpose is to steal, kill, and destroy (John 10:10). Here is how bloodline curses come about...

You inherit physical traits from your ancestors, such as eye color, hair color, intelligence, athleticism, etc. You also inherit generational influences such as physical and spiritual blessings or curses. The ability to recognize bloodline curses can alter the course of your life and change your destiny forever. For example, God blessed Abraham and his descendants with land, wealth, and victory over their enemies (see Gen. 12:1-2). He also placed generational curses on those who created and worshiped false gods and disobeyed His laws (see Deut. 5:9). Why generational curses? Because we inherit the iniquities, or sins of our ancestors. Iniquity means sin bent toward the next generation.[14]

Bloodline curses occur from the actions and decisions of our ancestors. If something happens once, that doesn't make it a curse. It must happen across at least two generations at the minimum. How do you know if your family has a bloodline curse? Look through the history of your family. Does domestic violence run through your family? What about cancer, high blood pressure, kidney stones, or diabetes? Do males die when they reach a certain age? Do members of your family suffer from depression or anxiety? What about addiction to porn, drugs, or alcohol? What pattern is occurring in your family?

In my family, my mom, sister, and I all got divorced. That is a bloodline curse. As I learned more about my grandmother and her family, I could pinpoint where that curse originated and how it started. It ran along the female side of my family and would have continued if it had not been stopped by the blood of Jesus.

The good news is Jesus cancels curses! We will talk more about this shortly. First, here are two lists to check out; one is a list of some of the root causes of curses found in the Bible, and the other is a list of Biblical curses resulting from those sins. Neither of these are exhaustive lists, but they are a good starting point for raising your awareness. It is essential to note the following Bible verse outlines the spiritual law: There cannot be a curse without a cause.

Proverbs 26:2 (NLT)

Like a fluttering sparrow or a darting swallow, an undeserved curse will not land on its intended victim.

Actions or sins that bring about curses:
Curses from our mouths (word cursing ourselves and others) (Prov. 18:21)
Stealing (Zach. 5:4)
Abortion (Ex. 21:22-23)
Pride (Ps. 119:21)
Idolatry (Ex. 20:5)
Depending on Man (Jer. 48:10)
Sexual perversion (Lev. 18:22-28)
Homosexuality (Lev. 20:13-16)

Premarital Sex (Deut. 22:13-21)

Incest (Gen. 19:36-38)

Treating the poor badly (Prov. 28:27)

Disrespecting parents (Deut. 28: 18-21)

Murder (ex. 21:12)

Disobeying God (Dan. 9:11)

Touching or owning cursed items (Josh. 6:18)

Adultery (Job 24:15-18)

Returning good for evil (Prov. 17:13)

Witchcraft (Ex. 22:18)

Fortune Telling (Lev. 20:6)

Horoscopes (Deut. 17: 2-5)

Symptoms as results of curses as explained in Deuteronomy 28:15-68:

Adultery

Alcoholism

Child abuse

Confusion

Depression

Destructive attitudes and behaviors

Divorce

Domestic violence

Drug addiction

Fear

Hereditary disease

Immorality

Indecision

Mental illness

Panic attacks

Perversion
Poverty
Sexual abuse
Sorcery
Suicide
Witchcraft

If you have identified a generational curse in your family, it is time to free yourself and your family from future casualties. You can break generational curses through the power of repentance, fasting, and the blood of Jesus. You can stand in the gap for your entire bloodline and allow Jesus to end personal and family pain and suffering.

How does the blood of Jesus cancel all generational curses? Remember, we operate under a spiritual, legal system. The blood of Jesus ends curses, much like a not-guilty verdict closes a court case. The blood of Jesus washes away the curse, and our bloodline is no longer guilty of the iniquity or sin that began the curse.

Unforgiveness, Anger, Hatred, Fear, Pride

Unforgiveness will open a door for Satan to enter. How so? It blocks our repentance. Satan hates repentance because repentance closes doors. Repentance eliminates Satan's legal access to operate in our lives. He must obey spiritual laws set by God. So, when you repent of your sin, evil can no longer afflict you since that door is closed. Now, you may still be oppressed due to other open doors, but not the one that was closed by repentance. You can ask the Holy Spirit to reveal hidden sin in your life to close doors you don't even know are open.

Jesus will not forgive our sins if we do not forgive others. It is another spiritual law. Matthew 6:14-15 states, *"If you forgive those who sin against you, your heavenly Father will forgive you. But if you refuse to forgive others, your Father will not forgive your sins.*" So, if you live with unforgiveness, you cannot be forgiven, and doors remain open. Therefore, anger and unforgiveness ultimately hurt you in the long run as they delay God's forgiveness of your sins.

The devil loves anger because it fuels unforgiveness. It is impossible to forgive someone and remain angry with them same time. You have two choices, forgiveness and anger. Depending on the circumstance, you have to decide upon which one you will act. That makes forgiveness a powerful weapon against the enemy! It packs a powerful punch.

I must mention that just because you forgive someone does not mean they will not receive or do not deserve a just punishment or consequence for what happened. It just means that you have released them into your freedom. You will no longer get triggered when you think about them or the incident. This can be hard, but it can be done by faith. Ask God to help you forgive when you cannot do it alone. He is faithful and will give you the grace to do so.

Unforgiveness and anger can lead to hatred. The Bible is forthright in telling us that in Gods eyes, hatred is akin to murder. 1 John 3:15 states, "*Whosoever hateth his brother is a murderer; and ye know that no murderer hath eternal life abiding in him.*"

Fear is a demonic spirit, not an emotion. When you start to feel fearful, you are discerning a demonic spirit trying to gain entry to your soul through an open door. The Bible says to resist the devil, and he will flee (see James 4:7). So, use the word of God as your weapon. Speak to fear out loud and command it to go in the name of Jesus! (There are spiritual warfare verses in Appendix B to memorize and wield, like a sword, when you feel the spirit of fear is near.)

Pride is having great satisfaction with yourself and your accomplishments.[15] Pride is what got the devil kicked out of Heaven. Satan thought he was better than God, so he was cast out of Heaven down to Earth. Pride will give the devil legal access to your life. Instead of feeling like you are better than everyone else, humble yourself before others or lower your importance compared to others.

COVENANTS

Do you know what an altar is? You have probably seen one at a church. An altar is where two or more spirits meet to form a legally binding agreement. Altars can be physical places, such as the altar in the church, or spiritual places that we cannot see with our five senses. Consider this: your desk where you sign the documents may serve as your altar when you sign a contract to buy a house. It is the actual location where two spirits unite to reach a consensus. In this case, your bank account may be another altar. Altars are places where two or more spirits meet to make an agreement.

There are altars at churches where two people meet to get married and make a legal promise to one another. When two entities, people or spirits, meet at an altar, they make an agreement, otherwise known as a covenant. A covenant is a legal agreement or promise that binds someone to something or someone. A covenant can only be broken through proper recourse to the laws set in place.

A sacrifice is always made when a covenant is formed at an altar. Thousands of years ago, the Israelites sacrificed their best animals to symbolize their allegiance to God (see Lev. 9:7 and Num. 6:14). In marriage, one sacrifices one's personal needs to care for and provide for another person; they agree to compromise.

Witches and warlocks also erect altars and make sacrifices on these altars to make promises and show their allegiance to false gods like the god of this world, Satan. (God is the Lord over all creation. Satan is just renting space here and will be evicted when God is ready to take back what is rightfully His.) A sacrifice always involves erecting an altar and making a covenant or agreement; something is offered on the altar in return for a desired result.

So, how does Satan separate us from God? One tactic is creating legal contracts, or covenants, with a person knowingly or unknowingly. You can make a covenant with either side of this battle. You can make legal promises to God or the devil. You can also create covenants on purpose or through sheer ignorance. However, you cannot have covenants with God and Satan simultaneously. There is no middle ground, and there is absolutely no mixture allowed. 1 Corinthians 10:21 states, *"You cannot drink the cup of the Lord and the cup of demons too; you cannot have a part in both the Lord's table and the table of demons."* Therefore, you must choose a side, ultimately determining where you spend eternity when you graduate from Earth School. Let's discuss several examples of covenants that can also fall into the "ignorance" and "disobedience" categories.

OATHS

There are numerous ways to make a covenant. You can verbally covenant with God by repenting, turning from sin, committing to serve Him alone, and abiding by His laws. God guarantees you a relationship with Him and an eternity in Heaven in exchange.

You can also make a verbal agreement with the devil. Remember, in any agreement you make with the devil, the sacrifice is your spirit. For example, several famous singers openly admit to making a "pact" with the devil.[16] They have exchanged wealth on Earth for their souls. Several of these music artists have even admitted that demons come out of them or even take over their bodies during performances.[17] No amount of money in the world would cause me to make that deal!

You can even make a covenant with the dark side and not even know it! An example would be taking an oath to join a secret society such as the Freemasons or a fraternity/sorority. Often, these oaths are taken at an altar. Usually, you are making a pledge, or promise, to a deity or the deceased founder. For example, in college, I joined a sorority. Upon our initiation into the sorority, we were asked to take an oath I have since broken.

Many politicians make covenants when they take oaths to serve God, other gods, or their country. Many politicians and even top executives of large businesses are in secret societies, the Freemasons being one of the most popular.[18] At the upper levels of the Freemasons are Luciferians, meaning they worship the devil or Lucifer whom they consider a god. Many of the founding members of our country and presidents were high-ranking Masons.[19] This is the same god mentioned on the back of the dollar bill…. the god of the Freemasons, who they call "The Great Architect of the Universe," or Lucifer.[19]

I don't want to get too far off-topic. Secret societies is a broad and comprehensive topic. Be careful when joining a "group," and never take an oath. Taking an oath is in direct disobedience to the Living God. Disobedience separates you from God and will make your life and others' lives susceptible to evil, curses, and unwanted sacrifices in areas such as health, wealth, relationships, your destiny, etc., by allowing the devil legal access to your soul.

WORSHIPING IDOLS

I think you will be surprised how easy it is to have idols. According to Webster's Dictionary, an idol is an object of "extreme devotion." I like to explain idolatry as anything you put before your obedience to God.

Some people think of idols as statues made of rock, clay, gold, silver, bronze, and copper, much like the statues of the ancient Greek gods or Egyptian Pharaohs. One recently erected statue in New York City is the Golden-horned statue of Medusa.[20] Medusa is a goddess of destruction, and someone thought it a good idea to place her in the center of the city of New York. So, although erecting idols still occurs today, it is becoming less common. The devil has gotten more sophisticated in how he traps people, unknowingly, into idol worship.

Social media is the new foundation for modern idol worship. Today's idols are likelier to be influencers on TikTok, Instagram, and YouTube or famous musicians, sports figures/teams, models, and politicians.

Now, you probably do not pray to these people. However, if you spend lots of time watching them, keeping up with their social media feeds, dressing like them, acting like them, talking like them, and hanging up pictures of them around room space, you've made them an idol. You know you have an idol if you are trying to copy their image to be like them.

Idols don't have to be celebrities. Idols can be anything you make more important than God. You can make your boyfriend or girlfriend an idol. Your problems can become an idol. Concepts such as evolution, careers, cars, money, the internet, your phone, your destiny, etc., can all become idols.

I always thought I was in good standing on this rule because I never had any statues of gods I worshiped. That right there is... you guessed it. Ignorance. I was guilty of this one on all accounts. I often would make myself an idol through vanity and selfishness. God killed this part of me when he placed me into a season of transformation. Since it's so simple to fall back into this trap, I have to actively work every day to avoid doing so.

In the last few years, people have made an idol out of deliverance or the casting out of demons. Many deliverance ministers are Godly people committed to winning souls and freeing people from demonic captivity.

However, the public has gotten so caught up with watching deliverance videos, traveling worldwide to attend deliverance conferences, and studying demons and methods to eliminate them out of their lives. Instead of worshiping and drawing closer to God, the Deliverer, they are placing a higher value on the act of deliverance. We need to worship the Deliverer and not the act of deliverance.

WITCHCRAFT AND THE OCCULT

Besides verbal covenants or agreements, there are also covenants made by engaging in rituals. For example, in Africa, it is very common for someone sick to see a local witch doctor. The witch doctor, known as an "herbalist," will restore their health with the help of demonic forces in exchange for something, which usually involves a bloodline curse. Sometimes, the sick person is asked to drink a potion or wear some trinket given by the witch doctor. In exchange for this item, the person must sacrifice something such as the wealth of future generations within their bloodline. So, the ill person gets well, and his children do not suffer the consequences of poverty. However, the grandchildren, great-grandchildren, and great-great-grandchildren on down the bloodline will experience poverty. The curse of poverty, in this case, can only be wiped out by breaking the covenant. Anyone in that bloodline can break this covenant through Christ. We will talk more about how to do so in later chapters.

Whenever you are asked to follow a set of directions precisely as prescribed, which may or may not make sense, to obtain a desired outcome, know that this ritual comes with evil attachments and sacrifices whether or not you realize it. So, the next time you want to ace your math mid-term and someone tells you to light two white candles and one green one, place them on the floor precisely two feet apart, and dance around them three times with your calculator in your pocket and a finger up your nose. Ugh, don't do it. The act of witchcraft will create a covenant between you and whatever evil spirit arrives to take you up on the offer. (Just for naysayers, this ritual is not real. I wanted to give you an example of what a ritual is, and help you understand that no matter how silly it may seem, it will produce devastating consequences.)

Witchcraft is partnering with evil for a desired result. A few examples of witchcraft include casting spells, the use of charms/crystals/stones, horoscopes, numerology, fortune reading, palm reading, tarot/oracle card reading, use of a pendulum, séances, and laying on of hands to manipulate auric field, chakra work, meditating to manipulate the spiritual realm to manifest in the physical realm, hypnosis, and astral travel.

Some people will tell you that there are different types of witchcraft, such as "white" magic or "black" magick. Do not be fooled; any form of witchcraft is a dance with the devil, regardless what term used. It is very simple; either you are engaging in witchcraft or you are not. Either you are partnering with evil, perhaps veiled as light, or not. You are either in rebellion or not. Don't let anyone deceive you by telling you there are good and evil witches. It is all the same underlying force at work... Lucifer and his army. Engaging in any of these activities, even just once, can open the door to evil, invoke a curse on your bloodline, and keep you and your bloodline oppressed.

Have you heard of the ice bucket challenge? This challenge was popular years ago when people would pour a bucket of ice water over their heads. Although the news media will deny this, the ice bucket challenge is a satanic ritual. John Ramirez, a former warlock now a great man of God, engaged in this ritual as the final step in his demonic initiation. He explains this challenge is a ritual in a high-ranking voodoo ceremony from Haiti called Sansi. This initiation into the highest level of witchcraft includes baptism with ice water, known as a demonic baptism.[21]

Please be careful when you see something going viral that everyone else is doing. Use discernment and research the origins of what they are doing before you join in. If the Lord tells you not to do it, don't do it. If you don't feel right about it, don't do it. It is not worth it.

My father was a prominent pathologist or one who studies diseases. He ran the Clinical Health Laboratories for one of the largest hospitals in the United States. He saw what went on behind the scenes and knew many secrets regarding the interplay of the medical and political worlds that he couldn't reveal tell us, but he always warned us not to be the first one to try something.

I will take his advice a step further and say, never follow the ways of the world. And if you are a Christian, you are not of this world. You are a citizen of the Kingdom of God; so stop doing what everyone else is doing. God has called you to be set apart from the world!

Games

Video games can open doors. Video games that feature bloodshed, violence, terror, sex, or witchcraft can provide easy access for the enemy to gain access to your life. Casting virtual spells in a gaming world is the same as casting spells in the real world. A spell is a spell regardless of where it is invoked and the intent behind it. I always hear, "I am just playing a game." The spiritual world reacts to the physical world. Period. If you cast spells in game mode, you will be accused by the devil of witchcraft.

Before I gave my life to the Lord, I would allow my son to play a video game filled with witchcraft. I am not joking when I tell you that bats would appear, out of nowhere, in his bedroom, and he would see shadowy figures all over the house. This game opened the door to the demonic realm. It gave demons legal access to our home. The door opened out of ignorance, as I did not know any of this when I allowed him to play that game.

There are other games, besides certain video games, that are demonic tools straight from the pits of hell. One of these is the Ouija Board. Early in 2023, a Ouija Board story made national news.[22] Twenty-eight girls were taken to the hospital after playing with a Ouija Board at school. The girls passed out after playing with the board and summoning demonic spirits. According to the hospital, the fainting could have been caused by "stress." However, you now understand that stress was not the cause; rather the children opened a demonic portal with the "game board." They came into a covenant or agreement with evil spirits, and this witchcraft opened a door for the devil to operate in their lives. Unfortunately, this covenant will remain intact beyond that one incident during school until the power of the Holy Spirit breaks it. I would even go a step further and say that the classroom and school building are accursed due to the operation of witchcraft.

This is not an isolated incident. There have been many news reports worldwide about children and teenagers getting struck with illnesses after playing with the board in school. The largest instance took place in Mexico City in 2006; 512 students were affected with illnesses and an inability to walk that would come and go.[23]

These games are no joke and should be avoided under all circumstances. Here is another one that took me by surprise. Satan is grooming young children at a very young age into the occult by selling toys that promote witchcraft. I was looking through a toy catalog the other day and noticed a plastic spell casting playset for children three years old! It comes with a plastic cauldron or pot, a book of spells, a magic wand, potion bottles, etc. The devil isn't playing; he is all business and pulling out every stop before his reign on earth comes to an end.

PREMARITAL SEX, FORNICATION, ADULTERY, PORNOGRAPHY

Sex is a spiritual act. Yes, it takes place physically, but it greatly affects the spiritual realm. At the very least, sex creates spiritual soul ties between people. A soul tie is when your mind, will, and emotions become attached to another person, place, or thing. God put laws in place to protect you from the spiritual implications of sex outside of marriage, adultery, pornography, and fornication. He flat-out tells us not to do it. I will leave it at that. (See Deut. 5:18 and 1 Cor.6:18)

ABORTION

If you have ever had an abortion, drove someone to an abortion, paid for someone to have an abortion, been the father of an aborted fetus, been a doctor or nurse performing abortions, voted, lobbied, or campaigned for abortion rights, or been involved in any way in the advising, planning, funding, preparation, or killing of a fetus you have made a covenant with the Spirit of Molech also spelled Moloch.[24]

Molech is the ancient god of child sacrifice; and even in Biblical times people would pass children through the fire of Molech in exchange for wealth, health, appeasing their gods, etc. (See Ezek. 16:21). If you have come into agreement with human sacrifice to this ancient heathen god, you are now connected to Molech both in the spiritual and physical realm. Leviticus 18:21 states, *"You shall not give any of your children to devote them by fire to Moloch and so profane the name of your God."*

This spirit now has legal rights to abort or kill off anything it wants in your life. It may do so right away or wait until a more opportune time. This spirit may choose to abort another child in your family, your life, your career, your finances, your relationships, your health, and the list could go on and on.

If you open a door to Molech, you need to repent. Not only have you broken God's rule not to commit murder, but you have also made a sacrifice to this ancient god. You will need to genuinely repent to God, renounce the abortion, your part in it, the spirit of Molech, and all other evil that gained access to your life through this sin, and replace the demonic spirit with the Holy Spirit of God under a new promise with Him. By the mercy of God, He will forgive you. How do I know? In His mercy, He forgave me.

Music, Lyrics, Spoken Words

Sound is energy in the form of waves that move through a medium such as air.[25] The waves are made of vibrating molecules. Sound waves can create or destroy in both the physical and spiritual dimensions. For example, when God created the Earth, He did so by saying out loud, *"Let there be light"* (See Gen. 1:3).

Scientists have tested the idea that sound creates physical forms and found that it is one hundred percent accurate. Cymatics is the study of visible sound vibration.[25] Scientists have found that different sound frequencies create different patterns, or formations, in sand or salt. The patterns create the same physical form each time the same frequency is played. I recommend watching the "Cymatics: Science vs. Music- Nigel Stanford" video on YouTube.[26] It is awesome. Nigel is a composer who shows the physical shape of sound by incorporating science experiments into his electronic music videos. This video is an excellent example of how a sound creates form. Watch this video right now, if you can, before reading further.

Well, what did you think of the video? Amazing, that sound can create formations!

Ok, let's move on. I am about to tell you another secret that every witch, warlock, and wizard on the face of the planet knows, but very few Christians genuinely understand.

Now that you understand vibrations from sound can create patterns, physical forms, objects, etc., let's think about the words we speak. When we speak, our words carry a specific vibration unique to each word or string of words we say. Those vibrations from our speech can create in the physical plane of existence or Earth. Your words quite literally create your reality. Therefore, our spoken words carry a great power to create or even destroy.

Dr. Emoto is a famous scientist who discovered water freezes in different crystalline structures when exposed to different words when spoken out loud, written on water bottles, or when exposed to varying types of music.[27] For example, he would speak a word to a glass of water and then freeze a few drops of that water to see what patterns the ice crystals would create. He found that when water was exposed to words such as "love" and "gratitude," the water would form into beautiful, intricate, and symmetrical ice crystals. However, when the water was subject to words such as "Satan" or "hate," the crystals were unsymmetrical and disorganized. In conclusion, the arrangement of water crystals was negatively affected by harmful speech, and they responded positively when exposed to positive and nurturing words.[27]

The human body is made of 60-70% water. So, how do the words we say affect one another? How can we apply the knowledge gained from Dr. Emoto's experiments? I wonder if Dr. Emoto is familiar with Proverbs 18:21 that states, *"Death and life are in the power of the tongue."*

So, we know that sound can create. We know that our speech has the power to create or destroy by way of sound. What about the music we listen to? Yes, Dr. Emoto's experiment was tested on heavy metal music such as Metallica and classical music. He found the results to be consistent with evil or kind spoken or written words. The water crystals looked nasty when exposed to heavy metal and beautiful when exposed to classical music like

Beethoven. You now understand the vibrations in music can be harmful, but what about the lyrics?

Any evil lyrics spoken begin to create things first in the spiritual world that could show up in the physical world. You can unknowingly invite evil spirits, take an oath, make a covenant to an evil spirit, or create unwanted trouble in the spirit realm through the lyrics you sing or agree with. This can happen knowingly or unknowingly, and why music can also fall under the ignorance category.

Yes, this does seem a little extreme, but it is spiritual law, and there is no way around it. Your words create, so be careful what you speak. You need to both choose and use your words wisely.

And just as words create, they can be used as weapons of spiritual warfare. The Word of God, when spoken out loud, can destroy, delay, disrupt, confuse the enemy, and cancel the enemy's plans. The Word of God is like a sword used to slay the enemy in battle and decree a new thing. (We will address this in detail later.)

DREAMS

One way God communicates with us is through dreams (see Job 33:14-15). He may give us instructions, tell us about future events, warn us, or bless us during our dreams. But remember, the devil mimics God and he cannot create anything new. Therefore, evil can also plant evil in our dreams. Godly and ungodly covenants can be made while we sleep, and we need discernment to know with whom we came into agreement (see Matt 13:24-30).

The topic of dreams could fill volumes of books. If you would like to know more, I highly recommend looking up Pastor Kevin L.A. Ewing on YouTube.[28] He is a Godly man who bases all of his teachings on dreams in biblical truth.

YOGA

In the language of Sanskrit, yoga means "to yoke" or to bind together.[29] Each pose in yoga is a physical movement designed to worship one of the hundreds of Hindu gods.[30] Just like we can worship God with song, we can also worship God with movement, dancing, etc. Yoga was a religion and a form of worship as each individual movement binds, or spiritually connects you, to one of the Hindu gods. These movements are evil covenants or agreements.

Yoga has become a form of exercise in America, and Hindus are unhappy about it. We took their religion and worship rituals and made them into a series of stretches and strengthening exercises; of course, they are offended.

I had a friend who loved yoga. She would often go on destination retreats to practice yoga or do so on her lunch breaks at work. She even started taking courses to become a yoga instructor. Over time, I noticed that she would get sick a lot. It began as a bad cold, then progressed into a series of staph infections, which are bacterial infections that are very hard to kill. And then, she got internal shingles, which are painful with no cure. She was getting so sick she couldn't work and had to take off several weeks at a time.

I started noticing a pattern. After each yoga retreat, she returned even more sick than the last time. The more retreats she attended, the more mysterious illnesses she would get without any root cause. Doctors were baffled but I wasn't.

I can tell you precisely what happened. She yoked herself to a spirit of infirmity, or sickness, by submitting to yoga and unknowingly creating a covenant with this spirit. She unknowingly opened a door through idol worship, by worshiping other gods through yoga.

People always say to me, "I don't practice yoga to worship other gods; I do it to stay in shape. It helps me relax." Listen, I must be honest. (I don't say this to sound harsh so please forgive me if it comes off that way.) The laws that govern the spirit realm will not take into consideration your motives for doing yoga. Yoga is what it was created to be, idol worship. If you do it; you open a door that will allow evil to access your life. I don't write this to incite fear, but to explain the spiritual implications in the hopes that you acquire clarity about some of the issues you've been encountering as they may relate to some of these practices.

Finally, churches, youth groups, teachers, preachers, pastors, and school leaders offering yoga, meditation, and mindfulness you are contributing to the Church to Cauldron Pipeline. I urge you to read the Letter to Leaders at the end of the book.

REIKI

Reiki is a trendy, New Age, hands-on, healing modality and alternative to traditional medicine. I spent years studying Reiki from several of the world's most famous Reiki healers. I wasn't just traveling the world taking random Reiki classes; I became a student of two prominent Reiki Masters. One of the women had written several books that are international best sellers and foundational in the New Age practice of the art of healing. Both of my teachers were instrumental in spreading Reiki across our culture; and both women were high-level witches.

I shouldn't have to explain any further for you to understand that Reiki is witchcraft, seeing as though two of the most famous Reiki healers on the planet are both witches. But I will tell you more in case that is not enough to convince you.

As a New Age practitioner, I learned to see in the spirit. However, when you enter the spirit realm any other way than through the Holy Spirit, you enter scary territory. All you can see is evil. Yes, you can see angels. But they are demonic beings disguised as angels of light.

I say all this because as I would facilitate Reiki for someone, I would always see a spirit standing next to that person. I saw what the New Age would call "divine mothers." I saw giant Samoans in fur clothing, little children, angels, choirs, and high priestesses, to name a few. The New Age will tell you these are "spirit guides" to assist you on your earthly journey. And they are spirits, alright...straight from the pits of Hell. I would see these spirits attach themselves to people during a Reiki session and leave with them after the session finished.

Yes, during Reiki, a portal is opened for demonic spirits to attach themselves to people. If you have ever had anything to do with Reiki, from taking a class to receiving Reiki, driving someone to Reiki, etc., you have come into agreement with witchcraft, and you most likely have company that followed you home. Seriously.

I don't say this to scare you. I tell you to warn you so that you can choose Jesus over Reiki and Yoga; and He will heal you. He will also separate you from any demonic oppression or evil covenant that you came into agreement with, knowingly or unknowingly upon repentance. This is one of the beautiful things about giving your life to Christ. The Son of God will set you free (see John 8:36). There is a prayer at the end of the book to break curses and several recommendations for books about deliverance and being freed from demonic oppression. Please be sure to check out the appendices.

OTHER NEW AGE PRACTICES

I have talked a lot about this in the previous pages. However, there are a few practices that I have not mentioned. These include meditation, automatic writing, shadow work (getting to know your "inner child,") and connecting with other entities through meditation.

Demons love a vacuum. Where there is a void, they will rush to fill it. This is why meditation is so dangerous. Many religions use meditation as a means to clear their minds and leave their physical bodies. Shamen are witch doctors who utilize mediation to journey through time. Even these witch doctors will tell you that evil can attach to your soul during mediation and follow you right out of the vision into reality. If witch doctors, who are clearly practicing witchcraft, admit this is true, why do people insist that meditation is harmless?

Several trendy influencers in the New Age movement have connected with groups of "beings" in the spiritual realm. These influencers will allow the "beings" to speak through them. These beings will talk about how to "raise your frequency" in order to make money. They will tell the future, give "helpful" advice, and direct you to your "soul purpose" in life. I'm here to reveal the truth to those who follow these influencers or attempt to connect with a group of these beings. The story below is a true story and will blow your mind.

Mark 5: 3-11 (NIV)

When Jesus got out of the boat, a man with an impure spirit came from the tombs to meet him. This man lived in the tombs, and no one could bind him anymore, not even with a chain. For he had often been chained hand and foot, but he tore the chains apart and broke the irons on his feet. No one was strong enough to subdue him. Night and day among the tombs and in the hills he would cry out and cut himself with stones.

When he saw Jesus from a distance, he ran and fell on his knees in front of him. He shouted at the top of his voice, "What do you want with me, Jesus, Son of the Most High God? In God's name *don't torture me!" **For Jesus had said to him, "Come out of this man, you impure spirit!"***

Then Jesus asked him, "What is your name?"

"My name is Legion," he replied, "for we are many." *And he begged Jesus again and again not to send them out of the area.*

A large herd of pigs was feeding on the nearby hillside. The demons begged Jesus, "Send us among the pigs; allow us to go into them." He gave them permission, and the impure spirits came out and went into the pigs.The herd, about two thousand in number, rushed down the steep bank into the lake and were drowned.

Influencers connected with these collective groups of spiritual beings have attached themselves to a "legion," meaning many demons. Do you want to know how many soldiers make up a legion; between 5,200-6,000 soldiers.[31] That means the man in the story above had over 5,000 demons tormenting him.

Those who follow these influencers are coming into agreement with witchcraft, divination, and fortune-telling; those who choose to "host" these beings have opened themselves up to the influence of thousands of demons.

I must mention one final thing: without repentance, New Age practices are a one-way ticket to Hell. The New Age will open the door for bloodline curses and evil covenants. I am not joking; avoid all New Age practices like they were Covid. You don't need them.

If you are a Christian, you have the God who created the Heavens and the Earth on your side. The same Spirit that parted the Red Sea and rose Jesus from the dead lives in you! He is the most powerful Person ever to exist; and He is eternal. The Holy Spirit is the only spiritual influence you will ever need. Read below to grasp what God is telling us. (**Warning:** Don't skip over the verses below. It is imperative you not only read them but compare your life to what they tell us. Your eternal life depends on it.)

Galatians 6:19-21 (NLT)

Now, the actions of the flesh are obvious; sexual immorality, impurity, promiscuity, idolatry, witchcraft, hatred, rivalry, jealousy, outburst of anger, quarrels, conflicts, factions, envy, murder, drunkenness, wild partying, and things like that. I am telling you now, as ***I have told you in the past, that people who practice such things will not inherit the kingdom of God.***

I am not sharing these things out of legalism or religiosity; nor am I sharing this information to glorify the devil. I'm letting you know about these things so you can spot evil when it masquerades as light, so you have a deeper understanding of how your choices affect the physical and spiritual worlds, and where you spend eternity. You can use this knowledge to walk in victory, free others in bondage, and defeat the enemy.

If you have come into agreement with an unwanted covenant, there is good news! Through Jesus, you can break these covenants by repenting and coming out of agreement with the covenant by giving Jesus rule, reign, and dominion over your life. If you would like to break the evil covenants operating in your life, there will be prayers in Appendix A and additional book suggestions in Appendix D to assist you in the process.

THE BATTLE WAS WON
BEFORE IT EVER STARTED

GROWING UP, I was exposed to many Bible stories, but they were always taught randomly with a "moral to the story," much like Aesop's Fables or a Bernstein Bears book. I was never shown how stories in the Bible were connected to a greater purpose or taught about their spiritual significance. I always gave a good eye roll when someone tried to tell me about the Bible. I thought it was boring, fragmented, outdated, and disconnected from modern times.

If you feel that way right now, I am about to blow your mind with amazing truths about the Bible that will have you begging to learn more. You will be shocked when you understand the big picture and the purpose for all that happened across time. I will take you 10,000 feet above and give you a bird's eye view of the Bible regarding spirituality and the realm of the spirit. I hope it will make a big difference in your understanding of God's word, the ensuing battle for your soul, and how to stand in victory.

I am going to start at the beginning of time when Lucifer, or Satan, was God's top-ranking angel, an anointed cherub that ruled over one third of the angels in Heaven. He was beautiful, and his name in Hebrew was Helel, which stood for "the shining one."[32] Over time, he grew very jealous of God and felt as though he should be God (see Isa. 14:12-15). Because of his pride, God cast Helel out of Heaven, and he fell to the earth like lightning (see Luke 10:18).

In Genesis 1:1, the very first verse in the Bible states, *"In the beginning, God created the Heavens and the Earth."* However, the next verse, Genesis 1:2 says, *"The Earth was without form and void, and darkness was over the face of the deep. And the Spirit of God was hovering over the face of the waters."* Huh? What happened between these two verses?

God is perfect; therefore, God's creations are perfect. He does not make mistakes. So, after He created the Heavens and Earth, some event must have taken place to cause darkness and a void on Earth. The event had to have occurred between the time of Genesis 1:1, *"In the beginning, God created the heavens and the earth,"* and Genesis 1:2, *"And the earth was a formless void and darkness covered the face of the deep."* Could this have been the time when Satan was cast out of Heaven? Because of this, scholars believe a tremendous galactic war occurred between Helel and God's angel armies. Helel was cast out of Heaven thousands of years before God created the Earth as we know it today, which starts in Genesis 1:3 and states, *"And God said, Let there be light."* The belief that thousands, maybe millions of years, passed between Genesis 1:1 and Genesis 1:3 is known as the "Gap Theory."[33]

After God created man, Satan grew very jealous because God made man in His likeness and had given man dominion, or rule, over all the Earth, including authority over Satan (see. Gen. 1:26-31). This angered Satan as man was given more authority and power than him. He went from being the highest-ranking angel in Heaven to the lowest-ranking spirit on Earth. From that moment on, Satan was on a mission to steal man's authority and separate man from his Creator.

Adam and Eve were perfect when God created them as they were made in the likeness of God. They were sinless and lived in the same dimension as God. They lived in harmony in the Garden of Eden; they were immortal and had all their needs met. God gave them dominion and authority over everything on Earth. They could go wherever they wanted in the Garden of Eden and eat whatever they wanted except the fruit from one tree. God specifically told Adam and Eve not to eat from the Tree of Knowledge of Good and Evil. If they did, they would die, meaning they would no longer have immortality (see Gen. 2:17).

Satan desperately wanted Adam and Eve's authority to rule over the world. He knew that getting them to disobey God would give him legal access to usurp or take over their authority. So, he devised a plan...

Satan disguised himself as a serpent and tempted Eve into disobeying God by eating fruit from the forbidden tree. Eve then talked Adam into eating from the tree, and he too disobeyed God. In that moment, when they both chose to go against God's warning, Adam and Eve gave their dominion over the world to Satan (see Gen. 3). Satan had become and still is the ruler of this "world" (see 2 Cor. 4:4).

It is essential to remember God created everything, even Helel. So, God has rule over everything, including over all the Earth and Satan. Satan is buying time on Earth, much like renting space, until God decides it is time to evict him and take back the Earth. Satan has dominion over everything you see in this "world," such as the culture, government, education, entertainment, business, religion, etc. But not for much longer! That is why you see so many global events occurring on a large scale. Satan knows his time is limited, so he is quickly advancing his army. He is on a mission to separate people from God and populate the fiery pit of Hell.

God cursed each of them that fateful day when the serpent, Satan, tricked Adam and Eve to eat from the fruit of the Tree of Knowledge of Good and Evil. However, God also made an incredible promise.

God cursed Adam and the ground, promising that Adam would have to, painstakingly, work the soil as his source of food. God made the ground produce thorns and thistles that would make farming for food

BATTLE FOR YOUR SOUL

labor intensive. The Lord also told Adam that he would labor for his food until he died, and his body would return to the ground from where it came. Adam was no longer immortal. Through sin, God sentenced him and all humanity to death (see Gen. 3:17-20).

God cursed Eve. Because she disobeyed God and ate the forbidden fruit, God cursed her and all women to endure painful childbearing. And since Eve led Adam to sin, the Lord gave Adam authority over Eve (see Gen. 3:16).

God also cursed the serpent above all livestock and beasts of the field. The snake was made to slither on his belly and eat dust for the rest of its days (see Gen. 3:14). God told Satan He would put enmity, or hostility, between Satan and women (see Gen. 3:15). God would also put hatred between Satan's offspring, or children, and Eve's future generations (see Gen. 3:16). God then told Satan that Eve's "seed," or offspring, would crush him! Meaning there would be someone born within Adam and Eve's bloodline that would defeat Satan (see Gen. 3:15).

From the moment Adam and Eve sinned against God, they gave their authority over to the devil and were cursed to death. God knew that He would have to create a way to redeem the souls of His people. He knew His people would need a Savior to defeat death. God knew the spiritual laws and decrees He put in place and strategically unfolded the most significant victory this world has ever seen!

This is how the battle was won before it even started. Remember, Heaven is a Kingdom, and God is the King. Therefore, whatever He says must take place. He cannot go back on his word. For example, He did not say, "Let there be light...wait... I take that back." No. God commanded there be light, and He separated the light from darkness. He did not go back on His word. He continued to create in order to counteract or balance the light with darkness (see Gen. 1:4-5).

Kingdoms on Earth are run the same way as they are in Heaven. A king, who runs an Earthly kingdom, creates laws. Once a king establishes a law or rule, he cannot rescind or take it back. He must make a new law to counteract or balance the one he desires to change. And God did just that. That day in the Garden of Eden, God cursed man to death. Yet, He planned to restore man's eternal life and crushing Satan simultaneously! So, although He condemned man to death in the physical world, God had planned on sending a savior, His only Son Jesus, who would be born of Adam and Eve's bloodline to redeem man's soul so that he could live in Heaven with Him for eternity! This is when the battle for souls began.

God would create a way for man to be saved and have everlasting life through the death and resurrection of His only son, Jesus Christ (see Isa. 7:14). The question becomes how many generations down the line, from Adam and Eve, would this Savior be born?

This is where it gets wild…

Satan planned to contaminate and eliminate the bloodline of Adam and Eve. He would ultimately spend thousands of years trying to end their bloodline by killing them all or, at the very least, contaminating the bloodline with his "seed." Satan's plan has always been to steal, kill, and destroy.

Satan could not fulfill his plot to assassinate the bloodline from which Christ would be born, so he had to call for help. He planned to use other angels who had fallen out of grace with God. These angels manifested on Earth as Satan's army. These fallen angels are often called the Nephilim.[34] The Nephilim started to breed with the women on the Earth, or the "daughters of men," and have babies (see Gen. 6:4). The Bible refers to the offspring of fallen angels as the Raphaim.[34] Except these babies were giants! Huge. Some giants were over twenty-five feet tall and had six fingers and toes! The Bible talks about the Nephilim being as tall as cedar trees or roughly 120 feet tall.[35] (see Amos 2:9)

(Let's pause the story for a minute. I wanted to mention that there is much proof that these giants existed. There have been complete skeletons found worldwide that prove their existence.[36] Even architectural structures prove Giants lived on the Earth at one time.[37] I hate to break it to you, but the Egyptians did not build the pyramids, as many associate the Nephilim and the Rephaim with the gods of ancient history.[37])

Satan's plan to contaminate the bloodline appeared to be working. These giants were ravaging man, teaching them forbidden knowledge and corrupting the bloodline simultaneously.[38] (When a baby is born, it carries a combination of both its mother's and father's blood. Women were having babies with the fallen angels which meant that the blood of the Rephaim was part human and part fallen angel, or demonic.) God knew if this continued, no one would be left of pure descent from Adam and Eve, from which Jesus could be born. Helel, indeed, thought he was winning.

And in those days, the Earth was filled with half-human, half-demonic giants. God was angry as they were teaching man things God did not want man to learn, such as idol worship, witchcraft, astrology, sorcery, weaponry, and war.[38]

God had enough; and He was so mad that in Genesis 6:5-7 He said, *"I will destroy man whom I have created from the face of the Earth, both man and beast...for I am sorry that I have made them."*

However, there was one man that God could trust, and his name was Noah. Noah was of pure descent from Adam and Eve. The giants had not corrupted his family bloodline as he was a man of great faith who was in right standing with God. God forewarned Noah, telling him that He would wipe out every living thing on Earth with a massive flood.

He allowed Noah 120 years to construct the ark (see Gen. 6:13-22). And as God had promised, He released water from the Earth's interior and produced rain that flooded the Earth for forty days and forty nights.

He brought a great deluge to destroy the giants and all the corruption and wickedness on Earth. He destroyed every living thing except for those who were on the ark, both humans and living creatures (see Gen. 7:23).

A lot was going on during the days of Noah that were displeasing to God. Satan had managed to corrupt a large portion of the bloodline and corrupt man. Some people speculate that man was even manipulating DNA during the days of Noah.[39] God had wished He never created man and wanted to "blot" out every living thing upon the Earth (see Gen. 6:5-22).

God had Noah build an ark to save his family and various animal species. The purpose of the flood was to wipe the Earth clean from man's wickedness and start new. However, somehow (and I won't get into this right now), giants continued to exist beyond the flood. How do I know? David killed Goliath, a giant, which occurred after the flood.

Noah lived to be 950 years old and was able to see his descendants fill the earth. From the time of Noah until the birth of Jesus, God used men to pave the way for the birth of Jesus. He strategically used men like Abraham, Isaac, Jacob, Moses, and David to ensure the bloodline was not corrupted by marrying and having children with someone from another tribe that worshiped Idols, practiced witchcraft, etc. As a reward, God promised His people land of their own if they followed His ten commandments and did as He instructed (see Gen. 12:1).

So why was God so harsh on His people at times? He loved them. He was paving the way for the birth of Jesus so that He could "crush" Satan once and for all and give man everlasting life. The everlasting life that was once Adam and Eve's until Satan tricked them into disobeying God. God's laws were to keep His people in righteous, holy, set apart, and safe from evil attacks. He wanted to keep evil doors shut to protect His chosen people and secure the bloodline for the arrival of Jesus.

Throughout the Old Testament, God would test His people, the Israelites. Many men in God's army were sent into battles to destroy wicked people who did not worship God and were filled with evil. God would discipline His people for not following the laws He set in place. At times, men did not listen to God, which put the bloodline of Adam and Eve in jeopardy. God would then curse His people as a punishment. These punishments would cause His people to repent and return to living a Godly life (see Exo., Lev., Num., Deut.).

Throughout the Old Testament, when God's people wanted to repent for their sins and regain their right standing with God, they would sacrifice or kill their best animals on an altar (see Num. 6:14). Why? Because in the spirit realm, blood is a currency much like paper money; Bitcoin, gold, or silver is a currency in the physical realm. Sacrificing their best animals to God was a way to apologize in hopes He would forgive them, and they could return to God's good favor (see Lev. 17:11). They would offer an animal's life in exchange for their own "spiritual" forgiveness known as atonement (see Heb. 13:11). Evil tribes, such as the Canaanites, would also build altars and make sacrifices to their false gods for this very same purpose (see 1 Kings 18). Blood sacrifices created a covenant, or promise, between those making the sacrifice and the God or gods they worshiped.

When Jesus was born, all of Heaven rejoiced because the first part of God's promise was fulfilled. He had sent the "seed" of Adam and Eve to crush Satan!

Jesus was tempted by many of the things mentioned earlier in this book throughout his life, yet He did not falter (see Heb. 4:15). He remained sinless in a sinful world. He also healed the sick. He delivered people from demons. He performed miracles like walking on water and feeding thousands of people with only two fish and five loaves of bread. But even more impressive than the supernatural signs and wonders He performed; Jesus loved us so much that He died on the cross so that God would forgive our sins. He willingly gave His life as a blood sacrifice (see The Gospel of Luke).

Jesus willingly became the sacrifice to save humanity from eternal death the moment He died on the cross. Because He was sinless, He was God's ultimate and perfect sacrifice. By shedding His blood, all sins have been forgiven. It is the new and everlasting covenant with God, meaning animal sacrifices are no longer needed. Jesus sacrificed himself to save every soul on earth from their sins, and He rose again, defeating death, so that we can live in Heaven with Him for eternity (see 1 Peter 1:3).

The second part of God's promise to crush the enemy was fulfilled! When Jesus died on the cross, He took all our sins with Him. His blood (currency) paid for our sins, and His resurrection defeated death! Satan lost the moment this new covenant was formed between man and God through Jesus (see Col 2:15).

Everlasting life was restored for every human being on Earth! Luke 23:25-26 state Jesus' last words before He died on the cross, *"It is finished. Father, into your hands, I commend my Spirit."* Jesus knew God's plan was a success and that every man, woman, and child could have everlasting life in Heaven through Him.

So why is there still a battle if Jesus has already saved our souls? Great question. Please allow me to explain.

Remember that salvation is only for those made in God's likeness, those with a spirit. Salvation is for humans only, as we were made in the likeness of God. Salvation is only for the sons (and daughters) of man (see Titus 2:11-12). Salvation is for those who confess with their mouths and believe in their hearts that Jesus Christ is the Son of God who was sent to Earth and died for their sins (see Rom. 10:9). Salvation is for everyone who asks Jesus to reside in their hearts; it is a covenant between Jesus and each individual person. It is only through a personal relationship with Him that we go to Heaven. There is no other god, magic potion, mantra, prayer, spell, or good deed will lead you to Heaven. Jesus stated in John 14:6, *"I am the way, the truth, and the life; no one comes to the Father except through Me."* To spend eternity in Heaven, you must believe in Jesus, confess that He is your savior, and live it out—bottom line.

Satan knows this. He also knows his time is limited as Jesus promised to come back to Earth, throw Satan and his army into an eternal lake of fire, and reign forever with every soul that has accepted Him as their Savoir. Satan only has one tactic left since Jesus reinstated eternal life for His believers. The only thing Satan can do now is attempt to steal souls and separate us from God. He tries to do this by keeping people from accepting Jesus as their Savior or leading them into sin. He wants to take as many souls as possible with him to the eternal lake of fire and this is why the battle for your soul ensues.

Remember, at the beginning of the book, I mentioned that there will be one decision that you will need to make that will determine where you spend eternity. Your decision will depend on your answer to this question: Where do you want to spend eternity? Heaven or Hell?

If you answered Heaven, today is going to be the first day of the rest of your life! You will be born again as a child of God, a new creation; forgiven and invited to have a personal relationship with the Lord. Follow the steps and speak the prayers **out loud**, below, to commit your life to Jesus:

1. Think about your life from the moment you were born until now. Forgive anyone or any situation in your life that you have not yet forgiven; this includes forgiving yourself.

We cannot ask God to forgive our sins if we are unwilling to forgive others. Forgiveness is a crucial step.

If you are having trouble forgiving, please pray this prayer. God will grant you grace, soften your heart, and, with His help, give you the courage to forgive.

> *Dear Jesus, Thank You for your mercy and forgiveness upon my life. I sincerely want to forgive (insert name) for (what they did to you), yet I am finding it difficult to forgive them. Please soften my heart and grant me the grace to forgive just as You have forgiven me. I thank You, Lord, for your help. From this day forward, I will prioritize forgiving others in my life. In Jesus' name, I pray, Amen.*

2. Read the following prayer to yourself first and come into agreement with it. Next, read the prayer **out loud** to God. It is essential that these words not only come from your mouth **but from your heart**. Your prayers must always be sincere, as God knows what is truly in our hearts.

> *Dear Heavenly Father, I come before You as a sinner. I am genuinely sorry for the sins I have committed. (List them out loud now.) Please forgive me. Father, I wholeheartedly believe that you sent your Son, Jesus, to die for my sins, and He rose from the grave to give me eternal life. Jesus, I ask You to come into my life and live in my heart. I give my life to You and promise to live my life in a way that pleases You. I and give you rule, reign, and dominion over my life. I love You. Thank You for becoming my Lord and Savior. In Jesus' name, I pray, Amen.*

Congratulations! You have not only made the most critical decision of your life, but, as a Christian, you are now a crucial part of the army of God. I advise you to find a secret place to pray and pray often. Jesus promises in John 10:27-28, *"My sheep hear my voice, and they follow me and I give unto them eternal life."* You will be able to have conversations with the Lord! Read the Bible daily, starting with the book of Luke. Start memorizing scripture. If you'd like, you could start by memorizing some of the warfare scriptures in Appendix B. Finally, connect with a church that preaches the full gospel and get baptized in water and filled with the Holy Spirit.

It is important to mention that although the blood of Jesus saves us, Satan will still try to access our lives. To be honest, he tries much harder on Christians than non-believers. Many Christians will struggle due to covenants, disobedience, and ignorance. You will need to remain vigilant so that the devil cannot gain access to your life; it will be important for you to remember the traps we spoke about earlier. (This was not a comprehensive list but a good start) Our redemption doesn't exempt us from these attacks but gives us the power to defeat them. It is now up to you to use the power and authority your Savior Jesus Christ bestowed upon you to wage war in the spirit realm and defeat the enemy.

Not sure how to engage in spiritual warfare? The next chapter will provide you with strategies to defeat the enemy.

Know Your Weapons

To win a battle, you need to understand what weapons you have at your disposal. You also need to understand the authority or weight, a Christian carries in the realm of the spirit and how to operate from this place when using these weapons. Christians have power and authority through Jesus. Think about it this way: the same Spirit who raised Jesus from the dead lives in us! The Bible even says that we are seated in Heaven with Jesus! We wear crowns! We are heirs of the Living God who created the Heavens and the Earth! I pray that you grasp the magnitude of what I am saying and walk in the authority Christ gave you through the shedding of His blood!

In this chapter, we will talk briefly about the following weapons of spiritual warfare:

1. Speaking The Word of God
2. The Name of Jesus
3. The Blood of Jesus
4. Wearing The Full Armor of God
5. Repentance
6. Fasting
7. Prayer and Praying in the Spirit
8. Obedience
9. Praise and Worship

SPEAKING THE WORD OF GOD OUT LOUD

Throughout childhood, I was taught to memorize Bible verses to get invited to Friday night's pizza party. I never really cared much for pizza, and the parties were boring, so I never thought it necessary to memorize Bible verses. I often thought, "Why would I need to memorize Bible verses when I could look them up in the Bible? Pointless."

I wish the church had explained how the physical world is directly connected to the spiritual world. I would have memorized the entire Bible had I understood the power that the Word of God holds. I listed a few powerful truths about the Word of God below. I think some of them will surprise you.

1. The Word of God is a spiritual sword. When spoken out loud, it tears the enemy to shreds. It cancels the enemy's plans. It paralyzes the enemy in the spirit realm so that it cannot manifest in the natural.

2. If you obey God's word, you keep the door closed to the enemy, and evil cannot operate in your life.

3. The Bible outlines all the spiritual laws, or how the spiritual realm operates, and explains how to live in the physical world yet operate from a Kingdom mindset.

4. The Word of God, when spoken out loud, releases blessings, abundance, and miraculous healing.

5. The physical world reacts to what is happening in the spiritual realm, and the spoken Word of God frames or creates that spiritual world.

In other words, everything that happens on Earth must form in the spiritual realm first.

These are only a few reasons that outline the importance of committing Bible verses to memory. The Bible clearly states the importance of speaking the Word of God. Even the enemy, including Satan, demons, witches, wizards, and warlocks know the power behind God's word.

Remember that the Bible outlines all spiritual laws. Understanding what occurs in the spiritual world when you either follow or break God's instructions is critical. If someone had told me this when I was a teenager, I would have made very different decisions. I will take a moment to explain this to you because I do not want you to perish for lack of knowledge.

When Jesus taught his disciples how to pray, He prayed for God's will to be done on Earth as it is in Heaven. In Matthew 6:10 Jesus prays, *"Your kingdom come, Your will be done On Earth as it is in Heaven."* Jesus taught us that what happens on Earth must first form in the realm of the spirit. Our decisions in the physical dimension have a ripple effect on the spiritual dimensions and vice versa. So, anything that happens on Earth must first form in the spiritual dimension.

Speaking the Word of God out loud carries a heavyweight in the spirit realm. Proverbs 18:20 states, *"Death and life are in the power of the tongue."* That means what we speak has a profound impact around us. Speaking the Word of God is like wielding a double-edged sword. It can tear down the enemy, uproot the enemy's plan, frame our physical reality, bring blessings, heal illnesses, answer prayers, strengthen our faith, etc.

The Words *"God said"* are written ten times in the book of Genesis chapter 1. *"God said, let there be light."* *"God said, let us make man in our image."* After every time God spoke, whatever He said took form and manifested in the physical realm. For example,

Genesis 1:3-4 (KJV)

And God said, Let there be light; and there was light. And God saw the light, that it was good.

When God speaks, both the spiritual and physical realms respond and obey. The word of God is alive. That means the words in the Bible breathe, they have life, they are living. It doesn't matter that the words were written hundreds of years ago; they are alive. God's Words move Heaven and Earth. Use them! Speak them over your life. Speak them over your family and friends. Speak them over your problems. Don't just speak them once. Speak them over and over again until your reality shifts into alignment with His words.

I knew from my days in witchcraft that words create our reality, which is why witches cast spells. Sadly, I never learned this in church. The Christian church never taught me that speaking the Word of God out loud has more power than any possible plan of the enemy. I have tested this repeatedly, and God's word has never failed me. How have I tested God's word?

I remind God of His word in prayer and as I go about my day. I don't remind Him because He forgot what He said. I remind Him because He promised His words would not return to Him void or without form. Isaiah 62:6 states, *"Put the Lord in remembrance of His promises, keep not silence."*

Recently, my son had a staph infection in his finger. The condition was getting worse and lasted for several weeks. He was on the second round of antibiotics when the Lord reminded me of the verse below.

John 15:7 (KJV)

If you abide in Me, and My words abide in you, ye shall ask what ye will, and it shall be done unto you.

I knew I had met the criteria of abiding in Christ and His words abiding in me, so per this promise, I could ask anything, and it would be done. So, I prayed, and I reminded God of this promises. I said, "God, you said, your word does not return to you void. And in John 15:7 you promised that If I abide in you and your words abide in me, I can ask anything it will be done. Father, in the name of Jesus, I ask that my son's finger be healed. I decree that through your promise, the infection will dry up immediately. I thank you, Lord, for your faithfulness. In Jesus name, Amen."

We woke up the following day and the infection was gone! That infection lasted three weeks, and two different rounds of antibiotics couldn't touch it. Yet, when the word of the God was spoken over his finger, the Lord dried up the infection and healed his finger overnight. The evil plan that the enemy had scheduled for my son was canceled. God's word canceled the enemy's assignment and ended the attack on his health. God's word is powerful! And God is faithful in keeping His promises.

Had I not known that Bible verse, I would have never prayed that prayer. Who knows what would have happened to my son. This is why we need to read and memorize the Bible. When we have verses committed to memory, the Holy Spirit will remind us of those in our time of need so we can use them like a spiritual sword!

If you are ready to start sharpening your sword with the word of God, I have included some of my favorite Bible verses in Appendix B. Memorize them, think about them throughout the day, and speak them out loud. Declare them over your life and remind God of His word during prayer. I look forward to hearing your testimonies of how God moved in your life through His promises you spoke out loud.

The Name of Jesus

The Word of God says that Jesus is the name above every other name. It says that every knee will bow to the name of Jesus.

Philippians 2: 9-11 (NLT)

Therefore, God elevated him to the place of highest honor and gave him the name above all other names, that at the name of Jesus every knee should bow, in heaven and on earth and under the earth, and every tongue declare that Jesus Christ is Lord, to the glory of God the Father.

The Lords disciples would heal the sick and cast out demons using the name of Jesus. Why? Because the name of Jesus has power. His name has so much power that even those who do not know Jesus will be use His name to cast out demons and heal the sick, as written in the following verses.

Matthew 7:21-23 (AMP)

"Not everyone who calls out to me, 'Lord! Lord!' will enter the Kingdom of Heaven. Only those who do the will of my Father in heaven will enter. On judgment day, many will say to me, 'Lord! Lord! We prophesied in your name and cast out demons in your name and performed many miracles in your name.' But I will reply, 'I never knew you. Get away from me, you who break God's laws.'

The name of Jesus holds great power. As the Lord was growing my Faith, or belief in things not seen, He was teaching me just how powerful His name combined with faith can be. The Lord gave me a dream of one of my sons. He was far away, in another location shrouded in smoke, coughing, unable to breathe. In the dream, my son called me crying, saying, "I can't breathe. I can't breathe." I woke up with tears streaming down my face as I knew my son was in trouble, but I could not reach him in the dream.

Several weeks later my son asked for permission to vacation in Florida with a friend and his family. Totally forgetting about the dream, I gave him permission to go. As he was packing, I heard the Lord say, "Speak to the waves." So, I did as the Lord had commanded. I started to speak to the waves along the beach where he was staying. I remember saying, "In the name of Jesus, I command the wave to cease. When Blake enters the water, the waves will be no more. In the name of Jesus, the waters will be calm, they will be safe, and they will be life-giving, and not life-taking." I had no idea why the Lord had told me to speak to the waves a few days before he left, but I did as He instructed, knowing that obedience brings protection and provision.

Before leaving, my son had a horrible feeling about going to Florida, and he even called me as he, his friend, and his friend's father, girlfriend, and children were pulling out of the driveway for their vehicle ride to Florida to tell me he didn't believe he should go. He felt uncomfortable asking the woman to pull over and let him out of her car, so he drove with them to Florida despite the Holy Spirit's conviction.

The journey from Ohio to Florida took around fourteen hours. My son called me about four hours in, stating that the car was filled with smoke because one of the adults had been chain smoking the entire trip. He was having trouble breathing because the vehicle was so smokey. I couldn't believe it; and in that instant, I remembered my dream.

The Lord was trying to warn me about letting him go on this trip, and I completely missed the warning. I told my Blake I would come to get him; no matter how far away he was, I would be there. He asked that I wait until he got to Florida, and he would let me know if he wanted to come home.

After we hung up the phone, I heard the Lord say, "Speak to the smoke." I thought I heard wrong, so I asked the Lord, "Speak to the smoke?" He said, "Yes." So, I started speaking to the smoke as the Lord told me. "In the name of Jesus, I speak to the smoke surrounding Blake. Depart from him now! In the name of Jesus, I separate the smoke from my son, now! The smoke shall not go near him, and in the name of Jesus, where he goes, the smoke shall not follow."

I got a call the following evening after Blake had spent the afternoon at the beach. He said, "Mom, it is so weird. There are no waves in the ocean. The water is so calm it is almost boring to swim." He further explained there had been twelve deaths over the last two weeks from the rough water, and now there were absolutely no waves. All I could say was, "Praise God." The Lord had me speak to the waves. And the water was calm through the name of Jesus and by faith. Faith can move mountains and obedience leads to protection and provision.

The story gets even more amazing. Remember how the Lord told me to speak to the smoke? That evening, Blake texted me, "The adults got in an argument and the woman is packing her bags to leave. Can you please come to Florida and get us because she is driving her smokey car home and leaving us here." The Lord had me speak to the smoke in faith, and the smoke separated itself from my son! I drove to Florida the next morning and brought Blake home with many lessons from the Lord.

Looking back, I should have never let my son go on that trip. The Lord had sent many signs from a dream, the hesitation He placed in Blake's heart, and the fact that my son was going with a couple that did not have a relationship with the Lord. The Lord kept Blake safe, strengthened my faith, and taught me the power that the name of Jesus holds.

The Blood of Jesus

Earlier in the book, you read about the blood of Jesus. When Jesus died on the cross and shed His blood, which is currency in the realm of the spirit, He washed our sins away. The Bible explains this law in Romans 5:17. *"If one man's sin can bring death to all (talking about Adam), then one man's righteousness (meaning Jesus) can save all from sin and death."* Sin separates us from God. But if we believe Jesus died for our sins, His blood speaks for us; it washes away our sins and reconnects us to God.

The blood of Jesus breaks curses and releases blessings. The Bible states that any man who hangs on a tree is cursed. Jesus was crucified on a wooden cross. Therefore, He became accursed for us, and the accusations, against us, were also nailed to that cross.

Galatians 3:13-14 (AMP)

Christ has redeemed us from the curse of the law, having become a curse for us (for it is written, "Cursed is everyone who hangs on a tree"), that the blessing of Abraham might come upon the Gentiles in Christ Jesus, that we might receive the promise of the Spirit through faith.

The blood of Jesus heals. Isaiah 53:5 states, *"By His stripes, we are healed."* The stripes are the lashings that Jesus took as they whipped Him and tore the flesh off His back before nailing Him to the cross.

The blood of Jesus sanctifies us, makes us holy, puts us in the right standing with God, and sets us apart from the rest of the world.

The blood of Jesus protects us. In the days of Moses, the Lord sent ten plagues to Egypt. The tenth and final plague was one of death. The firstborn of every household would die by morning. To protect God's people enslaved in Egypt, they were to place the blood of a lamb over their door-posts, and the angel of death would pass them over. It was a blood covenant made between God and His people. Exodus 12:13 states, *"When I see the blood, I will pass you over."* The blood of Jesus is the new covenant, and it protects Christians just as the lamb's blood did in during the Passover (see Ex. 11-19)

The enemy hates the blood of Jesus because it cleanses us from sin and reconnects us to God. The Bible tells us in Revelations 12:11, *"And they overcame him (Satan) by the blood of the Lamb (Jesus) and by the power of their testimony."*

My friend called me one day to tell me about some strange dreams she was having. One of the nightmares concerned me so much that I felt compelled to drive to her house right away. When I arrived, she was behaving strangely, and I could see she was concerned about having me at her house. She clearly did not want me there.

When we began discussing her nightmares, she eventually came forward to tell me that, three weeks earlier, a tall shadow figure had interrupted her sleep and had entered her body through her stomach. As she attempted to raise her head to pray, it held her head to the pillow until she fell back asleep.

I knew precisely which demonic spirit we were dealing with as it was one that I had personally encountered years prior. (Sleep paralysis is not a medical condition. It is a demonic spirit. If you are experiencing this, the Lord will set you free through deliverance.) It seemed somewhat odd that she wouldn't allow me to pray over her—this was a woman of God who was deeply in love with the Lord, read her bible every day, prayed frequently, prophesied, and served others. She informed me that because of the demonic attack, she was unable to pray.

I told her I was going to go to the corner of the room and pray quietly. Although she accepted that I could pray to myself, she insisted that we move to a more private area of the house because she thought her deliverance might become noisy. As we moved into the back room of the house, we put on music and I began to pray.

After a few worship songs, the Holy Spirit led me to speak over her, "In the name of Jesus, Incubus, come up and out of her now!" She began coughing and crying. The Holy Spirit led me to say, "She belongs to the Lord, and I saturate her now with the blood of Jesus." At that moment, she began vomiting as the spirit left through her breath. Demons hate the blood of Jesus, and it is a mighty weapon against the attacks from the kingdom of darkness.

There is protection in the blood of our Savior. Declare the blood of Jesus over yourself, your loved ones, your modes of transportation, homes, workplaces, schools, churches, careers, finances, health, and problems, over every doorpost of your life.

WEARING THE FULL ARMOR OF GOD

In the scripture below, the Bible explains how our enemies are not made of flesh and blood, meaning humans. Our enemies are evil spirits called principalities, powers, and rulers of the darkness. In order to stand against these enemies, we are told to put on the "full armor of God." We can pray for the armor to be on, but we must live out the armor. We cannot wear the pieces of armor that we do not live out with integrity. The armor of God is listed below.

Ephesians 6: 10-17 (AMP)

In conclusion, be strong in the Lord [draw your strength from Him and be empowered through your union with Him] and in the power of His [boundless] might. Put on the full armor of God [for His precepts are like the splendid armor of a heavily-armed soldier], so that you may be able to [successfully] stand up against all the schemes and the strategies and the deceits of the devil. For our struggle is not against flesh and blood [contending only with physical opponents], but against the rulers, against the powers, against the world forces of this [present] darkness, against the spiritual forces of wickedness in the heavenly (supernatural) places. Therefore, put on the complete armor of God, so that you will be able to [successfully] resist and stand your ground in the evil day [of danger], and having done everything [that the crisis demands], to stand firm [in your place, fully prepared, immovable, victorious]. So stand firm and hold your ground, having tightened the wide band of truth (personal integrity, moral courage) around your waist and HAVING PUT ON THE BREASTPLATE OF RIGHTEOUSNESS (an upright heart), and having strapped on YOUR FEET THE GOSPEL OF PEACE IN PREPARATION [to face the enemy with firm-footed stability and the readiness produced by the good news]. Above all, lift up the [protective] shield of faith with which you can extinguish all the flaming arrows of the evil one. And take THE HELMET OF SALVATION, and the sword of the Spirit, which is the Word of God.

Armor of God

Belt of Truth

Breastplate of Righteousness

On Your Feet: The Gospel of Peace

Shield of Faith

Helmet of Salvation

Sword of the Spirit, which is the Word of God

REPENTANCE

Earlier in the book, you learned how sin separates us from God. Sin opens a spiritual door that allows the devil to interfere in our lives and cause trouble. You also learned how God sent his only son, Jesus, to shed His blood, die on the cross, and rise from the dead after three days. When Jesus became a sacrifice on the cross, our sins were forgiven.

After we sin, we need to repent or turn away from our sin. Satan hates repentance because it brings us closer to God and shuts down his legal access to interfere in our lives. Repentance is more than telling God we are sorry. Repentance means we also try hard not to commit that same sin again. Repentance means coming out of agreement with or renouncing the sin completely. For example, you might say, "Heavenly Father, I repent of swearing and speaking poorly of others. I am truly sorry. Please forgive me. I renounce this sin and come out of agreement with using language that does not please you." Then you are mindful of not saying those things again.

It is essential to live a life of repentance to keep evil from entering through open doors of sin. That means to repent as soon as you realize you have sinned. Don't wait until bedtime to ask the Lord. You can ask Him for forgiveness right after you know you sinned.

Repentance is important, but the Bible takes it further in James 5:16, which says, "*confess your sins out loud to another and pray for one another that you may be healed.*" Confessing our sins out loud to another person can heal you! This is another excellent battle tactic for facing illness, depression, etc. Ask the Lord what sin opened the door to illness. Then, confess your sin to another, repent to the Lord, renounce the sin, remind God of his word in James 5:16, and claim your healing in the Name of Jesus!

FASTING

Fasting means to turn down your plate and go without eating for a specified period of time. Fasts can vary by length of time and what can and cannot be consumed. For example, some people will go on water-only fasts (water and no food) for several weeks. I have also gone on fasts that last for several hours each day—for example, abstaining from food from 6 am-6 pm for several days to even months. (It is always important to check with a healthcare professional before fasting. It is also essential to know how to break a fast or come off a fast so as not to cause physical harm when returning to a regular diet.)

Fasting brings us closer to God, brings about miracles and blessings, and is a spiritual warfare tactic. Many Christians will fast when they are experiencing health concerns, financial concerns, relationship struggles, wanting to grow closer to God, seeking God for an answer to prayer, wanting to break a curse or seek deliverance, etc.

There is more to fasting than turning down your plate. During a fast, we substitute physical food for supernatural food, meaning the Word of God. Whenever you get hungry, read the Bible and pray. Isaiah 58 gives directions on how to fast in a way that will please the Lord. If you are interested in fasting, I suggest reading that chapter of the Bible before your fast.

It is important to feed the hungry, give to the less fortunate, and provide for those in need during a fast. The Bible also says that we are not to tell anyone about our fasting or else public recognition will be the only reward we receive. We are rewarded for what we do in private; keep the fast between you and the Lord. Isaiah 58 warns against complaining during a fast as well.

Fasting will also allow the ugliness inside of you to bubble to the surface. It might reveal anger, sadness, fear, bitterness, unforgiveness, pride, idolatry, or another sin that is need of repentance. During this time, bad behaviors usually get worse as the Lord shows you what needs to be addressed and removed from your life. The enemy in the spiritual realm will most likely attempt to prevent you from obtaining your blessing, which will result in spiritual battle in both your dreams and real life.

PRAYER AND PRAYING IN THE SPIRIT

Prayer is powerful, and praying out loud is even more powerful. Reminding God of his Word during prayer is still even more powerful! Having Faith when we pray can move mountains! I have seen the power of prayer dissolve cancerous tumors in seconds, turn the word curses of doctors into misdiagnoses, place money in bank accounts that had no origin, restore marriages, remove demonic oppression, cast out evil spirits, break curses, redirect storms, and restore vision to name a few. Prayer is a spiritual weapon!

Jesus promises in Matthew 18:19, *"Again, truly I tell you, if two of you agree on earth about anything you ask, it will be done for you by my Father in Heaven."* So, there is power when we come together and pray in agreement with one another. The Bible also says in Deuteronomy 32:30, *"One will put 1000 to flight, two will put 10,000 to flight when God is on our side."* When we pray in accordance to God's will, we are shooting targeted missiles in the realm of the spirit that change the course of events in the natural world; nuking the plans of the Enemy and setting in motion the plans of God.

A spiritual warrior must also have a secret place to pray, a prayer closet. This is where you spend time alone with the Lord. You can talk with Him privately, pour your heart out to him, praise Him, receive guidance and direction, read your Bible, and receive revelation from the Holy Spirit. Your prayer closet is also your battle arena where you will pray for others, intercede, and dismantle the enemy. It is in this place where the Lord will shelter you and hide you from the Enemy. Because you have been hidden in the shadow of the Almighty, your spiritual enemies will be unable to locate you. You have got to read this Bible verse. It will blow your mind away!

Matthew 6:6 (AMP)

But when you pray, go into your most private room, close the door, and pray to your Father who is in secret, and your Father who sees [what is done] in secret will reward you.

You can enter "the secret place" whenever you want, as many times a day as you would like, especially when the Lord tells you. Often, the Lord will wake me up in the middle of the night and call me into prayer. Sometimes, it is hard to wake up, but obedience is important, and there is a life depending on it.

When I started praying in the secret place, the Lord would wake me up in the early hours of the morning to pray very specific prayers. Early one morning, around 1 a.m., I was called into prayer and waited for the Lord to speak. (This takes patience and persistence as sometimes you can wait an hour or more for Him to speak.) The Lord startled me with a vision I was not expecting. He showed me a man walking into the grocery store who had stopped to look at flowers. He was wearing a red hat, a white long-sleeve shirt, and a zip-up vest. The Lord proceeded to instruct me to be at the grocery store at 10 a.m. and pray a prayer of healing over the man.

Since this was the first time the Lord had given me a stranger to approach and pray for hours before it was supposed to happen, I initially believed I was making this up. I prayed to the Lord for an indication that He was speaking; and I asked God to give me a reason to go to the grocery store if these instructions were indeed from Him. When I woke up several hours later, I received a phone call from my mother asking me to stop at the grocery store to buy extra sausage for breakfast. We never eat sausage. I knew that the Lord had orchestrated this call from my mom to confirm my assignment.

Needless to say, I got in my car drove to the grocery store to meet the man in the red hat and long-sleeved white shirt. As I parked my car in the lot, I realized I had gotten there early as it was 9:45 a.m. In that moment, I heard the Lord say, "He is early; hurry up and get into the store and stand in front of the apples so you can see him walk in." I was so eager to go inside that I neglected to lock the doors. "There isn't time," the Lord stated as I turned around to lock my car door. "Leave your car unlocked and go inside."

As I walked into the grocery store and stood in front of the apples, I turned to watch who was walking in through the automatic sliding glass doors. Just as I turned to the door, a man with the red hat, long-sleeved white shirt, and zip-up vest walked in and stopped to look at the flowers. The scene was just as the Lord had shown me in the vision during prayer.

My heart was pounding as I had never approached a stranger in public with a word from the Lord and a commission to pray. "This is going to sound crazy...but the Lord sent me here to pray with you," I remarked to the man. The man had a strange smirk on his face, as if he knew something I didn't. I continued, "Last night, the Lord gave me a vision of you walking in the store, wearing the exact outfit you have on now. He told me I was to pray for healing. Is this resonating with you?"

The man said, "Yes. My wife was just recently given a scary diagnosis. And this isn't crazy at all. I have had several strange encounters this morning leading me to this store. I would like for you to pray with me."

I could hear the Lord telling me to tell him, "The Lord says that you have been praying for a divine appointment and that although this was not the appointment you were expecting, it was the appointment He had planned for you."

The man grinned and indicated that he had been trying to arrange an appointment for his wife to see a doctor as soon as possible, and that this was the type of appointment he had been hoping for. He did receive the appointment, but the Lord also desired that He receive this supernatural appointment for prayer.

We prayed together in the grocery store for all to see. We prayed for his wife, for her healing, and an increase in their faith. That day, we agreed on healing, set 10,000 to flight, and believed the Lord healed his wife. I never heard from him after that day, but I am confident God used that encounter to plant seeds of faith and bring healing. Every time I go to that grocery store, I look for him and pray that one day we will reconnect so he can share his testimony.

While the man and I prayed in our native language, it is also possible to pray in a Heavenly spiritual language. The Holy Spirit gifts you with tongues when you get filled or baptized, with the Holy Spirit. Mark 16:17 states, "And these signs shall follow them that believe; In my name they cast out devils; they shall speak with new tongues." When you are filled with the Holy Spirit He will give you a new language and He will intercede, or pray on your behalf, when you speak in tongues. When you feel as though you no longer have the stamina to pray or are unsure of what to pray, use this Heavenly language. Romans 8:26 explains, "In the same way, the Spirit helps us in our weakness. We do not know what we ought to pray for, but the Spirit himself intercedes for us through wordless groans."

OBEDIENCE

Obedience to the Lord leads to blessings and protection. The Bible goes as far as saying obedience is better than sacrifice (see 1 Sam. 15:22). If the Lord urges you to do anything, don't put it off. Do what He says and in the time frame He specifies. There's a valid explanation behind this.

Often, the Lord will provide me with a prophetic word for someone else, but it will also be for me. One day, I took my son, Logan, to look at a car. We walked into the Mazda dealership, met a car salesman, test-drove one car, and left with his business card in hand. That night in prayer the Lord gave me a prophetic word for the car salesman that started something like this, "Return the money! Return the money! Return the money! Return the money!" I kept hearing the Lord repeat this phrase over and over. I sat on the word when the Lord completed imparting the full message. I was terrified to call and tell salesman the Lord's word.

The word of the Lord began to weigh on me; it was all I could think about, and it became a huge burden that I couldn't bear any more. After several days of trying to keep the message to myself, I found the courage to call the Mazda dealership and ask for the salesman, only to get his voice-mail. As the Lord did not want me requesting him to return money on his work voice mail, I opted to text his personal phone number, which was also listed on his business card. I released the message from the Lord including the rebuke about returning the money, and anxiously awaited a response. I didn't hear back from him.

The following day, he called me and explained that he was going to pay his back taxes that morning and thanked me for relaying the message from the Lord. Because he and I obeyed the Lord, it kept him from getting in trouble with the IRS. But the story doesn't stop there!

My oldest child, Logan, was struggling to find employment. Although every local business was hiring, he was landing interviews yet not getting hired. I knew it was a spiritual blockage, but I couldn't figure out the root cause. The Lord continued to weigh on me about the message of "Return the money!" Even after telling the car salesman, I continued to carry a personal burden as a result of the word. I was aware that it implied that I owed money somewhere.

I tried to remember if I'd ever stolen money before, even as a child. I'd always been against stealing and couldn't bring myself to take something that wasn't mine. The Lord then reminded me of a day when I was fifteen and a friend and I were babysitting for a family I had known for three years. My friend wanted to take money from a large stack of cash that she found. I continued to refuse her requests until I could no longer stand the peer pressure. Although the exact amount of money she had stolen is beyond my memory, I am aware that it was a few hundred dollars.

The Lord instructed me to give the family their $300 back as soon as possible. Even though the money had been stolen thirty-two years prior, the Lord still wanted me to shut that door. I waited three days to act upon what the Lord had told me to do. As He began to reveal the urgency of the matter, I finally repented, renounced, and confessed to the family what I had done as a teenager. I wrote them a letter in which I described what had happened thirty-two years before. I apologized and left my current phone number as well as $300 cash. The next day, the woman called me, and we had a beautiful talk, remembering and catching up on lost time. She appreciated my letter and was very forgiving.

Do you know what happened three hours after I returned that money? My son was offered two jobs! He had gone months with many interviews and not one single job offer. As soon as I obeyed the word of the Lord and "returned the money," my son didn't get just one job but two! He got to choose which position he wanted! In the secret place, the Lord heard my prayer about Logan's situation and answered the prayer because of my obedience.

It may be your disobedience that is causing your prayers to go unanswered. Go back and complete the last task that God gave you instructions on if you find yourself asking Him for your next course of action, what to do, or your next assignment and He is not responding. He may not be asking you to "return the money" but He has asked you to do something. Your disobedience may be the root cause of the silence you are experiencing.

PRAISE AND WORSHIP

Psalm 100:4 states, *"Enter into His gates with thanksgiving and His courts with praise."* Remember, Heaven is a Kingdom. In prayer, giving thanks to God is the key to entering the gates of the Kingdom of Heaven. We then enter into the courtyard of Heaven with praise.

Praise and worship is another powerful weapon. While we praise and worship God, He inhabits our praises and gives us strength to defeat our enemies. Worship as opposed to worrying. Give Him thanks and praise for things that the natural world hasn't yet seen. Your praise will go before you and God will fight your battles.

The word "praise" has Semitic roots in the Akkadian Language.[40] The Akkadian were a fearsome and warring people who used the word praise in reference to "shooting an arrow." Instead of hand-to-hand combat with the enemy, you can shoot from a distance with praise! Remember this when you don't feel like praising. When all you want to do is worry or give ground to fear and sadness. Begin to thank God for what He has done, though it has not yet appeared in the physical realm. Choose to praise Him instead of giving ground to worry; shoot arrows into the realm of the spirit and let the Lord go to battle for you!

Let The Spirit Of Truth Set You Free

In Hosea 4:6, God says, *"My people perish for lack of knowledge."* Who are "His people?" Christians, and they are perishing because they lack knowledge. Please read this next verse...it is a sobering verse, and if it doesn't put the fear of God in you, I don't know what will. One reason Christians are perishing due to lack of knowledge is not realizing the spiritual consequences of the actions listed in this scripture. Do any of these actions apply to choices you are currently making?

Revelations 21:8 (AMP)

But as for the <u>cowards</u> and <u>unbelieving</u> and <u>abominable</u> [who are devoid of character and personal integrity and practice or tolerate <u>sexual immorality</u>], and <u>murderers</u>, and <u>sorcerers</u> [with intoxicating drugs], and <u>idolaters</u> and <u>occultists</u> [who practice and teach false religions], and all the <u>liars</u> [who knowingly deceive and twist truth], their part will be in the lake that blazes with fire and brimstone, which is the second death."

There are countless numbers of Christians engaging in acts listed in this verse; and I was one of them. Listen to me...there are no excuses in Heaven. It does not matter if you did not know that engaging in Yoga "to relax" was practicing a false religion. It does not matter if you did not realize that using meditation to manifest money is an occult practice. It does not matter if you did not understand that idol worship is putting anything before your obedience to God. It does not matter that you did not know that all the little white lies you were telling were a big deal in the courtroom of Heaven. It doesn't matter that you thought having sex outside of marriage was okay because you were in love. Your excuses won't matter.

If you are practicing anything listed in Revelations 21:8, knowingly or unknowingly, it is time to repent and make the necessary changes in your life. You must be willing to make sacrifices in this life to spend eternity in Heaven. Jesus explains...

Matthew 7:12-14 (Amp)

Enter through the narrow gate. For wide is the gate and broad and easy to travel is the path that leads the way to destruction and eternal loss, and there are many who enter through it. But small is the gate and narrow and difficult to travel is the path that leads the way to [everlasting] life, and there are few who find it.

Proverbs 6:16-19 (KJV)

These six things the Lord hates, Yes, seven are an abomination to Him: A proud look, a lying tongue, hands that shed innocent blood, a heart that devises wicked plans, feet that are swift in running to evil, a false witness who speaks lies, and one who sows discord among brethren.

I pray that as you finish this book, you evaluate your life. What changes do you need to make to get on the narrow path? Commit to staying on that path, no matter what it costs you in the physical realm. Use the weapons God has given you to keep your soul (mind, will, and emotions) from falling prey to the Enemy. The battle for your soul is real, and eternity is a long time to be separated from God. Choose to stand in the authority God has given you and battle from this position of victory.

The Church To Cauldron Pipeline

A Letter for Church Leaders and the Body of Christ

Before you dive into this letter, I ask that you please do me one favor. Just as you would take off an old, worn pair of shoes at the door of your home, please set aside the spirit of offense before you read any further. Commit to reading first to understand. When offense starts to rear its ugly head, use your God-given authority to cast it down in the Name of Jesus. Please read this letter intending to be a part of the solution instead of perpetuating the problem. Thirty-three percent of the US population (and many more worldwide) need your attention, understanding, and ability to accurately reflect, repent, renounce, and rebuild as if their lives depend on it- because they do.

If you read my testimony in the first few chapters of this book, you will better understand what the Lord has coined, "The Church to Cauldron Pipeline." The suppression of the Holy Spirit in Church is leading God's sheep, who are hungry for the physical manifestation of God, straight into the occult pipeline and the "spiritual but not religious" (SBNR) sector. According to recent Fetzer[41] and Gallup[42] studies, thirty-three percent of the US population alone categorize themselves as SBNR. SBNR is an alphabetical cacophony for one whom the occult has snared due to offense and intense hatred for the spirit of religion.

You may be thinking that "spiritual but not religious" is a good thing. According to a recent Barna study, eighty percent of the SBNR population loves Jesus.[43] This sounds amazing! They love Jesus, so what is wrong? They love an SBNR version of Jesus. Their mindsets follow a doctrine of self because they have not had access to biblically-based spiritual discipleship. How am I qualified to speak about SBNR as a whole? I used to be an SBNR and walked in this identity for years. I got to meet and know hundreds of SBNRs. Here is what I learned about the SBNR pattern of thinking…

They no longer trust the church. They seek encounters elsewhere because they yearn for the tangible presence of God, which they have not encountered in the church. They are lukewarm, practice mixture, and are unknowingly involved in occult or New Age practices. They have created their religion and serve a Jesus they imagine in their minds. Their love for this Jesus is genuine; however, the Jesus they serve is a perverted perception of Jesus. The SBNR Jesus is tolerant; he does not judge, accepts everyone and their lifestyle, gives everyone what their hearts desire, moves parallel with self-actualization, and advocates for personal destiny. The "SBNR Jesus" is not Jesus of Nazareth, the Son of the Living God. It is a distorted version of Jesus serving present worldviews that shift as belief systems change and the level of "collective consciousness" rises. The SBNR Jesus is a false god.

At one time, I considered myself spiritual but not religious, and I loved the "SBNR Jesus" too. Ezekiel 34 explains my testimony shared in the first several chapters of this book. Please take a moment to read Ezekiel 34 carefully, as it will set the groundwork for what happened to me and a third of the US population. As you begin to read, I pray that the Holy

Spirit softens your heart and begins to speak to you through the Word of God and throughout this letter.

Ezekiel 34 (AMP)

And the word of the LORD came to me, saying, "Son of man, prophesy against the shepherds of Israel. Prophesy and say to them, the [spiritual] shepherds, 'Thus says the Lord GOD, "Woe (judgment is coming) to the [spiritual] shepherds of Israel who have been feeding themselves! Should not the shepherds feed the flock? You eat the fat [the choicest of meat], and clothe yourselves with the wool, you slaughter the best of the livestock, but you do not feed the flock. You have not strengthened those who are weak, you have not healed the sick, you have not bandaged the crippled, you have not brought back those gone astray, you have not looked for the lost; but you have ruled them with force and violence. They were scattered because there was no shepherd, and when they were scattered they became food for all the predators of the field. My flock wandered through all the mountains and on every high hill; My flock was scattered over all the face of the earth and no one searched or sought them."

Therefore, you [spiritual] shepherds, hear the word of the LORD: "As I live," says the Lord GOD, "certainly because My flock has become prey, My flock has even become food for every predator of the field for lack of a shepherd, and My shepherds did not search for My flock, but rather the shepherds fed themselves and did not feed My flock; therefore, you [spiritual] shepherds, hear the word of the LORD: 'Thus says the Lord GOD, "Behold, I am against the shepherds, and I will demand My flock from them and make them stop tending the flock, so that the shepherds cannot feed themselves anymore. I will rescue My flock from their mouth, so that they will not be food for them."

For thus says the Lord GOD, "Behold, I Myself will search for My flock and seek them out. As a shepherd cares for his sheep on the day that he is among his scattered flock, so I will care for My sheep; and I will rescue them from all the places to which they were scattered on a cloudy and gloomy day. I will bring them out from the nations and gather them from the countries and bring them to their own land; and I will feed them on the mountains of Israel, by the streams, and in all the inhabited places of the land. I will feed them in a good pasture, and their grazing ground will be on the mountain heights of Israel. There they will lie down on good grazing ground and feed in rich pasture on the mountains of Israel. I will feed My flock and I will let them lie down [to rest]," says the Lord GOD. "I will seek the lost, bring back the scattered, bandage the crippled, and strengthen the weak and the sick; but I will destroy the fat and the strong [who have become hard-hearted and perverse]. I will feed them with judgment and punishment.

"And as for you, My flock, thus says the Lord GOD, 'Behold, I judge between one sheep and another, between the rams and the male goats [between the righteous and the unrighteous]. Is it too little a thing for you that you [unrighteous ones who are well-fed] feed in the best pasture, yet you must trample down with your feet [of wickedness] the rest of your pastures? Or that you drink clear [still] water, yet you must muddy with your feet [of wickedness] the rest [of the water]? As for My flock (the righteous), they must feed on

*what you trample with your feet and drink what you muddy with
your feet!"'*

*Therefore, thus says the Lord GOD to them, "Behold, I Myself will
judge between the [well-fed] fat sheep and the lean sheep. Because
you push with side and shoulder, and gore with your horns all those
that have become weak and sick until you have scattered them away,
therefore, I will rescue My flock, and they shall no longer be prey;
and I will judge between one sheep [ungodly] and another [godly].*

*"Then I will appoint over them one shepherd and he will feed them,
[a ruler like] My servant David; he will feed them and be their
shepherd. And I the LORD will be their God, and My servant
David will be a prince among them; I the LORD have spoken.*

*"I will make a covenant of peace with them and will eliminate the
predatory animals from the land so that they may live securely in
the wilderness and sleep [safely] in the woods. I will make them
and the places around My hill (Jerusalem, Zion) a blessing. And I
will make showers come down in their season; there will be [abun-
dant] showers of blessing (divine favor). Also the tree of the field will
yield its fruit and the earth will yield its produce; and My people
will be secure on their land. Then they will know [with confidence]
that I am the Lord, when I have broken the bars of their yoke and
have rescued them from the hand of those who made them slaves.
They will no longer be prey to the nations, and the predators of the
earth will not devour them; but they will live safely, and no one
will make them afraid [in the day of the Messiah's reign]. I will
prepare for them a place renowned for planting [crops], and they*

*will not again be victims of famine in the land, and they will not
endure the insults of the nations any longer. Then they will know
[with assurance] that I the LORD their God, am with them and
that they, the house of Israel, are My people," says the Lord God.
"As for you, My flock, the flock of My pasture, you are men, and I
am your God," says the Lord GOD.*

What about Ezekiel 34 speaks to you as it relates to the Church to
Cauldron Pipeline? What was the Lord revealing to you as you read
this chapter?

If you are a leader in today's church, this may be a challenging chapter
of the Bible to read. However, I ask that you embrace the following word
from the Lord with humility and through the lens of the life of service from
which you have been called. In Ezekiel 34, the Lord calls for the return of
His scattered sheep. In order to retrieve the missing one-third of the US
population and stop the funneling of people worldwide into false doctrine,
we need to address the Church to Cauldron Pipeline.

We can no longer settle for "having a form of godliness yet deny the
power thereof." The Bible tells us to avoid that practice, which is precisely
what the SBNR sector have done. In their silent outcry for the presence
of the Holy Spirit, they have turned their backs to the church because
it has denied the move of the Holy Spirit. The SBNR have drifted away
from the church and toward false doctrine which is a perilous place to be
for both the SBNR and the ministries that are aiding in the dispersal of
The Lord's sheep.

When the Lord told me I was to use my testimony to further expose
the "Church to Cauldron Pipeline," in my carnality, I believed He was
speaking solely about Shepherds and the Westernized church leading
people to seek spiritual experiences outside of the move of God due to the

suppression of the Holy Spirit. Little did I know there was more to the pipeline that He would reveal. As the Lord highlighted Ezekiel 24, I could feel the palpable anger of the Lord.

Have you ever felt the anger of the Lord? Not the conviction of the Holy Spirit. Not the fear of the Lord. Have you felt the palpable anger of the Lord? It's paralyzing; that is the best way I can describe it. After the Lord revealed what I am to share with you next, I sat for hours, unable to speak under the weight of his anger and the power of His words.

I heard the Lord say, "An eye for an eye, Ezekiel 24 for Ezekiel 34, a cauldron for a cauldron."

(Before I further explain what the Lord wanted me to share, I must be honest with you. I went Moses on the Lord, asking, "Why me? Why am I the one to share this? Are there not others more qualified? Are there not others with a greater following to get this message out?" The Lord answered and said, "Those are the reasons; you are the one to share this message. You have no ministry. You have no following. You have nothing to fear and nothing to lose. I will get this message in front of the right people.")

So, with nothing to fear and nothing to lose, I pray that as you read Ezekiel 24, the anger of the Lord rests upon you as it did me. I pray His anger fuels you to make midcourse corrections and embrace the call to action that will retrieve His scattered sheep.

Ezekiel 24 (AMP)
The Parable of the Boiling Pot

Again in the ninth year [of King Jehoiachin's captivity by Nebuchadnezzar of Babylon], in the tenth month, on the tenth [day] of the month, the word of the LORD came to me, saying, "Son of man, record the name of the day, this very day. The king of Babylon has laid siege to Jerusalem this very day. Speak a parable against the rebellious house [of Judah] and say to them, 'Thus says the Lord GOD,

"Put on a pot; put it on and also pour water into it;

"Put in it the pieces [of meat],
Every good piece (the people of Jerusalem), the thigh and the shoulder;
Fill it with choice bones.

"Take the choicest of the flock,
And also pile wood under the pot.
Make it boil vigorously
And boil its bones in the pot."

'Therefore, thus says the Lord GOD,
"Woe (judgment is coming) to the bloody city,
To the pot in which there is rust
And whose rust has not gone out of it!
Take out of it piece by piece,
Without making any choice.

"For her blood [that she has shed] remains in her midst;
She put it on the bare rock;
She did not pour it on the ground
To cover it with dust.

"That it may cause wrath to come up to take vengeance,
I have put her blood [guilt for her children sacrificed to Molech]
on the bare rock,

That it may not be covered."

'Therefore, thus says the Lord GOD,
"Woe to the bloody city!
I will also make the pile [of wood] high.

"Heap on wood, kindle the fire,
Boil the meat well [done]
And mix in the spices,
And let the bones be burned.

"Then set the empty pot (Jerusalem) back on the coals
So that it may be hot
And its bronze may glow
And its filthiness may be melted
And its rust (scum) may be consumed.

"She has wearied Me with toil,
Yet her great rust has not left her;
Her thick rust and filth will not be burned away by fire [no matter
how hot the flame].

"In your filthiness are lewdness and outrage.
Therefore I would have cleansed you,
Yet you were not [willing to be] cleansed,
You will not be cleansed from your filthiness again
Until I have satisfied My wrath against you.
I the LORD have spoken; it is coming and I will act. I will not
relent, and I will not have compassion and I will not be sorry; in

accordance with your ways and in accordance with your deeds I will judge and punish you," says the Lord GOD.""

With nothing to fear and with nothing to lose, I will be the mouthpiece for the Lord and say again, "An eye for an eye, Ezekiel 24 for Ezekiel 34, a cauldron for a cauldron."

The Church to Cauldron Pipeline is a two-way street. If a church continues to feed its sheep into the Cauldron Pipeline, so will the Lord feed the church into a boiling pot, just as he did Israel in the parable of Ezekiel 24.

As I studied Ezekiel 24, I heard the Spirit of the Lord say, "If my sheep are herded into the Cauldron, so will be the shepherd that leads them there. Now is the time for repentance. Repent to the congregation. Turn from your evil ways. Reinstate the fear of the Lord in your midst, and I will expand your church outside the four walls of its captivity, for My hand has kept it from expanding."

And For those who will not listen to the word of the Lord, I heard Him say, "I will shut the door to your church in this season, and you will be no more. I will save My sheep by My hand. I will raise others from dust and ashes to bring forth the needed change in the church. This is a clarion call for My remnant to arise and heed the word of the Lord. Do what I have asked of you, and you will replace the leaders in your midst that have herded My sheep into the Church to Cauldron Pipeline to become meat devoured by the beast."

The fury of the Lord pours out like fire. Because we have allowed the spirit of religion to silence the Holy Spirit and restrain spiritual discipleship, sheep are fed into the occult. Because of the pressure from the fear of man, biblical truths that are uncomfortable to vocalize but need to be heard are omitted. The Lord is furious.

Romans 1:10 states, *"For the wrath of God is revealed from heaven against all ungodliness and unrighteousness of men, who by their unrighteousness suppress the truth."* Be honest with yourselves…What truths are you suppressing? The move of the Holy Spirit? Biblically-based spiritual discipleship? The authority Christians hold through Christ? The power of the blood of Jesus? The truth of the Lord concerning the LGBTQ community? The entrance of Babylon into your church?

It is not by chance that you are reading this letter; the Lord has specifically directed your attention to these pages. He is asking, "Will you be the solution?" On behalf of His scattered sheep, I ask that you seek the Lord in prayer. Ask Him to reveal what truths your ministry is suppressing and the root cause of that suppression. Is it the fear of man, the fear of cancel culture, or the fear of the admission of fault?

The Spirit of the Lord says, "Is not the fear of the Lord greater than these?"

Humble yourself before the Lord, as He will reveal the truths you have suppressed in this hour. Repent, and He will help you rebuild. "Your latter shall be greater than your former," says the Spirit of the Lord. "Remain silent, and the hammer of the Lord will crush your foundation into pieces."

As you finish reading this book, I lament with the heart of Jeremiah in verse 13:17, *"But if you do not listen to it, my soul will weep in secret for such pride; And my eyes will shed and stream down tears, because the flock of the Lord has been taken captive."*

I pray over you now. Father, Jeremiah 33:3 states, *"Call to me and I will answer you and tell you great and unsearchable things you do not know."* Father, in the name of Jesus reveal the breaches in the walls of the church that are funneling sheep into the Church to Cauldron Pipeline. I humbly ask that the Ruach of God rests upon every leader that reads this letter; shed Your light on the changes You are calling them to make in their ministries and in their walk with You. Grant them the wisdom needed to make crucial pivots in this season. Reveal Your heart to them, Father, that they may guide Your sheep in truth. May they train Your flock to be spiritual warriors that recognize when the predator is near and equip them to fight from a place of victory in Christ. May their churches walk in the fullness of Christ; that Your sheep will no longer wander astray. And Father, as they make shifts in their ministries, may they move forward with boldness and surety that they are walking in obedience and in accordance with Your will. In the mighty name of Jesus, I pray. Amen.

Appendix A

Prayers

Commit Your Life to Christ

1. Think about your life from the moment you were born until now. Forgive anyone or any situation that has occurred in your life that you need to forgive. This includes forgiving yourself.

   We cannot ask God to forgive our sins if we are unwilling to forgive others. Forgiveness is a crucial step.

   If you are having trouble forgiving, please pray this prayer. God will grant you grace, soften your heart, and, with His help, give you the courage to forgive.

   Dear Jesus, Thank you for your mercy and forgiveness upon my life. I sincerely want to forgive (insert name) for (what they did to you), yet I find it difficult to forgive them. Please soften my heart and grant me the grace to forgive just as you have forgiven me. I thank you, Lord, for your help; going forward, I will prioritize forgiving others. In Jesus' name, I pray, Amen.

2. Read the following prayer to yourself first to come into agreement with it. Next, read the prayer out loud to God. It is essential that these words not only come from your mouth **but from your heart.** Your prayers must always be sincere, as God knows what is truly in our hearts.

> *Dear Heavenly Father, I come before you as a sinner. I am genuinely sorry for the sins I have committed. (List them out loud now.) Please forgive me. Father, I wholeheartedly believe that you sent your Son, Jesus, to die for my sins, and He rose from the grave to give me eternal life. Jesus, I ask you to come into my life and live in my heart. I give my life to you just as you gave your life for my sins. I promise to live my life in a way that pleases you. I give you rule, reign, and dominion over my life. I love you, Lord. Thank you for becoming my Lord and Savior. In Jesus' name, I pray, Amen.*

A Warring Prayer For Healing

Dear Heavenly Father,

1. Enter into His gates with thanksgiving (see Psalm 100:4).

    I thank You for being a faithful and promise-keeping God. I thank You that Your words do not return to you void. I thank You for…(continue to thank Him).

2. Enter into His courts with praise (see Psalm 100:4).

    I bless You, Lord. There are no other gods above You. You are the King of Kings, and Lord of Lords, I praise the God of all creation, For You are matchless, there is none like You…(continue to praise.) Read Psalm 144 if you would like.

3. Father, In Matthew 18:19-20 you promised, *"Again, truly I tell you that if two of you on earth agree about anything they ask for, it will be done for them by my Father in Heaven. For where two or three gather in my name, there am I with them."* So, as we gather in Your name, we welcome the Holy Spirit to fill every crack and crevasse of this room. Lord, may Your Spirit be palpable that we feel Your presence with us. (Wait for the Holy Spirit)

4. Your Word says in Isaiah 54:17," *No weapon that is formed against thee shall prosper; and every tongue that shall rise against thee in judgment thou shalt condemn.*"

5. In Luke 10:19 Your word states, *"Behold, I give unto you power to tread on serpents and scorpions, and over all the power of the enemy: and nothing shall by any means hurt you."*

6. And in Matthew 16:19 Your word also states, *"I will give you the keys to the kingdom of Heaven, and whatever you bind on Earth shall be bound in Heaven, and whatever you loose on earth shall be loosed in Heaven."*

7. So in the mighty name of Jesus, I rebuke the spirit of infirmity over (insert name). I bind the spirit of infirmity now, in the name of Jesus! I command that spirit of (name spirit) to come up and out now. In the name of Jesus, your assignment has been canceled. You have failed. You have been served a cease and desist. You loose them now, in the name of Jesus.

8. Father, your Word says that when we decree a thing, it shall be established. I decree that by the blood of Jesus and His eternal covenant, every legal access Satan had over (his/her) health is nullified Now, in the name of Jesus.

9. Father, your Word also promises that Jesus became accursed for us. We thank You, Jesus, for becoming a living sacrifice for us. For it is by Your blood that every evil verdict levied against (insert name)'s health by ancestral or bloodline curses be eternally paralyzed in the realm of the spirit and no longer viable to operate in (their) life or the life of their family. The blood of Jesus cancels those curses, and the verdict stands as not guilty. In the name of Jesus, I break every word curse the doctors have spoken over (insert name), and those words fall dead to the ground now!

10. God, You are a God of order. Everything you make is perfect and in perfect order. So, in the name of Jesus, I declare order and restoration return to (insert name)'s body. I declare order to (their) DNA, cells, tissue, organs, and organ systems and declare full body restoration. I decree a new season for (insert name). A season of health and prosperity. I declare that everything that the enemy stole from (them) be returned sevenfold per the Word of the Lord. Whatever was stolen, be returned now in the name of Jesus!

11. The Word of God states in Jon 22:28, *"Thou shalt also decree a thing and it shall be established unto thee and the light shall shine upon thy ways."* So, in the name of Jesus, I declare that sickness will no longer be found when (insert name) returns to the doctor. I decree (insert name) will defy all odds, and the doctors, friends, and family will be baffled by the excellent report and a clean bill of health. They will say, "How did this happen? How is this possible?" And (insert name) will respond, "Jesus healed me, and from head to toe, I am fully restored." I decree in the name of Jesus, YOU WILL TESTIFY!!!

12. Thank You, Lord, that we can move mountains with faith the size of a mustard seed. Thank You, Lord, for casting this mountain into the sea. Thank you, Father, for Your Living Word, grace, mercy, and everlasting goodness. We give You all the glory. In the matchless name of Jesus, amen.

A PRAYER TO BREAK BLOODLINE CURSES

Please note that deliverance may require fasting and prayer; as Jesus said in Matthew 17:21, *"This kind does not go out but by prayer and fasting."*

Make a list of the curses that run in your bloodline. You can refer back to the curses section to determine which ones are evident in your family. If unsure, rely on the Holy Spirit to reveal them to you. Go to the Lord in prayer. Remind him of Jeremiah 33:3, which states, *"Call to me, and I will answer you and tell you great and unsearchable things you do not know."*

Dear Heavenly Father,

1. Enter into His gates with thanksgiving (see Psalms 100:4).

    I thank You for being a faithful and promise-keeping God. I thank You that Your words do not return to You void. I thank You for…(continue to thank Him).

2. Enter into His courts with praise (see Psalms 100:4).

    I bless You, Lord. There are no other gods above You. You are the King of Kings, the Alpha and Omega, I praise the God of all creation, For You are matchless, there is none like You…(continue to praise.) Read Psalms 144 if you would like.

3. Father, In Matthew 18:19-20 you promised, *"Again, truly I tell you that if two of you on earth agree about anything they ask for, it will be done for*

them by my Father in Heaven. For where two or three gather in my name, there am I with them." So, as we gather in Your name, we welcome the Holy Spirit to fill every crack and crevasse of this room. Lord, may Your Spirit be palpable that we feel your presence with us. (Wait for the Holy Spirit)

4. Your Word says in Isaiah 54:17," *No weapon that is formed against thee shall prosper; and every tongue that shall rise against thee in judgment thou shalt condemn."*

    In Luke 10:19 Your word states, *"Behold, I give unto you power to tread on serpents and scorpions, and over all the power of the enemy: and nothing shall by any means hurt you."*

    Father, in Jeremiah 33:3 you said, *"Call to me and I will answer you and tell you great and unsearchable things you do not know."* I ask You now, Lord, to reveal any bloodline curses running in my family and the root cause of those curses. Please reveal to me what Satan is bringing in front of the courts of heaven and holding against my ancestors. (Wait to hear what the Lord reveals if you do not know what curses run in your bloodline.)

5. Lord, my family is guilty of (List all sins that brought about the curse out loud.) I have forgiven my family for these sins. I ask You, Lord, in the name of Jesus, please forgive them for these sins. I also ask You, Lord, to forgive me where I have also committed or contributed to these sins. I am so sorry, Lord. Please forgive me. I renounce this sin and come out of agreement with it now!

6. Father, Your word states that Jesus became accursed for us because every man that hangs on a tree is cursed. And we know that the blood of Jesus speaks better things than that of Abel's.

    Your word also says in Colossians 2:14-15, that Jesus through his death and Resurrection *"was blotting out the handwriting of ordinances that was against us, which was contrary to us, and took it out of the way, nailing to his cross. And having spoiled principalities and powers, he made a show of them openly, triumphing over them in it."*

    I ask for the blood of Jesus to speak on my behalf and cleanse me of this sin, And that every generation back to the first mothers and fathers on both my maternal and paternal sides of my bloodline be acquitted, justified, and no longer guilty as Jesus shed His blood on the cross that we would stand acquitted in the courtroom of Heaven.

7. Now I speak to the spirit of (Name the spirit or curse. For example, the spirit of infirmity, the spirit of cancer, the spirit of depression, the spirit of death, the spirit of anger, etc.) I bind you in the name of Jesus. According to spiritual law, you no longer have legal rights to operate in my life, family, or bloodline. I command you to leave me, now, in the name of Jesus. For the blood of Jesus has set me free. The blood of Jesus has set my bloodline free. We stand acquitted in the courtroom of Heaven. So I now serve you a cease and desist. You must vacate our lives now!

    The Word of God states in Jon 22:28, *"Thou shalt also decree a thing and it shall be established unto thee and the light shall shine upon thy ways.*" So, in the name of Jesus, I decree my family has been set free from this curse. And I declare a physical manifestation of the breaking of this curse now! For whom the Son sets free is free indeed! Father now that the door to this iniquity has been closed, I ask in the name of Jesus, that all demonic oppression and consequences resulting from this curse be lifted and canceled and that I walk into the blessings and destiny You have preordained for me before the foundations of the world.

8. You can now pray the healing prayer above if the broken curse was about physical, mental, or emotional illness.

9. Father, thank You for being a covenant-keeping God. I thank You that Your words do not return to You void! Thank You for Your faithfulness. And thank You, Father, for the freedom we have in Christ. In the mighty name of Jesus, I pray, amen.

PSALM 91 FOR PROTECTION

[1] He that dwelleth in the secret place of the most High shall abide under the shadow of the Almighty.

[2] I will say of the LORD, He is my refuge and my fortress: my God; in him will I trust.

[3] Surely he shall deliver thee from the snare of the fowler, and from the noisome pestilence.

[4] He shall cover thee with his feathers, and under his wings shalt thou trust: his truth shall be thy shield and buckler.

[5] Thou shalt not be afraid for the terror by night; nor for the arrow that flieth by day;

[6] Nor for the pestilence that walketh in darkness; nor for the destruction that wasteth at noonday.

[7] A thousand shall fall at thy side, and ten thousand at thy right hand; but it shall not come nigh thee.

[8] Only with thine eyes shalt thou behold and see the reward of the wicked.

[9] Because thou hast made the LORD, which is my refuge, even the most High, thy habitation;

[10] There shall no evil befall thee, neither shall any plague come nigh thy dwelling.

¹¹ For he shall give his angels charge over thee, to keep thee in all thy ways.

¹² They shall bear thee up in their hands, lest thou dash thy foot against a stone.

¹³ Thou shalt tread upon the lion and adder: the young lion and the dragon shalt thou trample under feet.

¹⁴ Because he hath set his love upon me, therefore will I deliver him: I will set him on high, because he hath known my name.

¹⁵ He shall call upon me, and I will answer him: I will be with him in trouble; I will deliver him, and honor him.

¹⁶ With long life will I satisfy him, and shew him my salvation.

Appendix B

Bible Verses For Spiritual Warfare

Prepare for battle and sharpen your sword!
All verses are from the King James Version
(KJV) Bible unless otherwise marked.

John 3:16

For God so loved the world that He gave His only begotten Son, that whoever believes in Him should not perish but have everlasting life.

Romans 10:9

If you confess with your mouth the Lord Jesus and believe in your heart that God has raised Him from the dead, you will be saved.

Luke 10:19

Behold, I give unto you power to tread on serpents and scorpions and over all the power of the enemy; and nothing shall by any means hurt you.

Ephesians 6:12

For we wrestle not against flesh and blood, but against principalities, against powers, against the rulers of the darkness of this world, against spiritual wickedness in high places.

1 John 4:4

Ye are of God, little children, and have overcome them; because greater is he that is in you, than he that is in the world.

Matthew 18:19-20

Again I say unto you, that if two of you shall agree on earth as touching anything that they shall ask, it shall be done for them of my Father which is in heaven.

For where two or three are gathered together in my name, there am I in the midst of them.

John 15:7

If ye abide in me, and my words abide in you, ye shall ask what ye will, and it shall be done unto you.

Romans 8:37

In all these things we are more than conquerors through him that loved us.

2 Corinthians 10:4-5

For the weapons of our warfare are not carnal, but mighty through God to the pulling down of strongholds.

Casting down imaginations, and every high thing that exalteth itself against the knowledge of God, and bringing into captivity every thought to the obedience of Christ.

Colossians 2:14-15

Blotting out the handwriting of ordinances that was against us, which was contrary to us, and took it out of the way, nailing to his cross.

And having spoiled principalities and powers, he made a show of them openly, triumphing over them in it.

Matthew 16:19

"…And I will give you the keys of the kingdom of heaven, and whatever you bind on earth will be bound in heaven, and whatever you loose on earth will be loosed in heaven."

Mark 16:17

And these signs shall follow them that believe; In my name shall they cast out devils; they shall speak with new tongues;

They shall take up serpents; and if they drink any deadly thing, it shall not hurt them; they shall lay hands on the sick, and they shall recover.

Revelations 12:10-11

…The accuser of our brethren is cast down, which accused them before our God day and night.

And they overcame him by the blood of the Lamb, and by the word of their testimony, and they loved not their lives unto death.

Isaiah 55:11

So shall my word be that goeth forth out of my mouth; it shall not return unto me void…

Proverbs 18:21

Death and life are in the power of the tongue; and they that love it shall eat the fruit thereof.

Galatians 3:13

Christ hath redeemed us from the curse of the law, being made a curse for us: for it is written, cursed is everyone that hangeth on a tree:

James 2:19

Thou believest that there is one God; thou doest well: the devils also believe, and tremble.

Matthew 10:7-8

And as ye go, preach, saying the kingdom of heaven is at hand.
Heal the sick, cleanse the lepers, raise the dead, cast out devils: freely ye have received, freely give.

John 8:36

If the Son therefore shall make you free, ye shall be free indeed.

Matthew 7:7-8

Ask, and it shall be given to you; seek, and ye shall find; knock, and it shall be opened unto you;
For everyone that asketh receiveth; and he that seeketh findeth; and to him that knocketh it shall be opened.

Job 22:28

Thou shalt also decree a thing, and it shall be established unto thee...

Jeremiah 33:3

Call to me and I will answer you and tell you great and unsearchable things you do not know.

Matthew 17:20 (NIV)

Truly, I tell you, if you have faith as small as a mustard seed, you can say to this mountain, "Move from here to there," and it will move. Nothing will be impossible for you.

Isaiah 53:5

But He was wounded for our transgressions, He was bruised for our iniquities; The chastisement for our peace was upon Him, and by His stripes we are healed.

Romans 6:14

For sin shall not have dominion over you, for you are not under law but under grace.

Psalms 18:2

The Lord is my rock and my fortress and my deliver;
My God, my strength, in whom I will trust;
My shield and the horn of my salvation, my stronghold.

John 10:10

The thief does not come except to steal, and to kill, and to destroy. I have come that they may have life, and that they may have it more abundantly.

Matthew 28:18-20

And Jesus came and spoke to them, saying, "All authority has been given to Me in heaven and on earth.
Go therefore and make disciples of all the nations, baptizing them in the name of the Father and of the Son and of the Holy Spirit,

Teaching them to observe all things that I have commanded you; and lo, I am with you always, even to the end of the age." Amen.

Deuteronomy 11:24
Every place on which the sole of your foot treads shall be yours…

Deuteronomy 28:7 (AMP)
The Lord will cause the enemies who rise up against you to be defeated before you; they will come out against you one way, but flee before you seven ways.

Psalms 8:6
You have made him (man) to have dominion over the works of Your hands; You have put all things under his feet.

John 14:13-14
And whatever you ask in My name, that I will do, that the Father may be glorified in the Son.
If you ask anything in my name, I will do it.

Matthew 24:35
Heaven and earth will pass away, but My words will by no means pass away.

Isaiah 61:3
To console those who mourn in Zion,
To give them beauty for ashes,
The oil of joy for mourning,
The garment of praise for the spirit of heaviness;
That they may be called trees of righteousness,

The planting of the Lord, that He may be glorified.

Isaiah 40:31

But those who wait on the Lord

Shall renew their strength;

They shall mount up with wings like eagles

They shall run and not be weary,

They shall walk and not grow faint.

Matthew 15:13-14

But He answered and said, "Every plant which My heavenly Father has not planted will be uprooted.

Let them alone. They are blind leaders of the blind. And if the blind leads the blind, both will fall into a ditch."

Appendix C

Additional Resources

Books

Deliverance From Demonic Covenants and Curses, by Rev. James A. Solomon.

The Bible-Based Dictionary of Prophetic Symbols, by Dr. Joe Ibojie

YouTube Channels

Tomi Arayomi (Founder of RIG Global Church)

Nathanial Bassey's Hallelujah Challenge (21 days of praise and worship)

Pastor Kevin LA Ewing (Biblically based teaching on spiritual warfare and dreams)

Global Prophetic Alliance (Emma Stark)

NOTES

1. Gary, Pastor. "Resisting the Enemy – Pastor Gary Snodgrass." *Christian Center Church*, 1 May 2018, christiancenter.us/ resisting-the-enemy-pastor-gary-snodgrass.

2. Tomi Arayomi. "GOD SAYS WE ONLY HAVE NINE YEARS | 2021 PROPHECY | Tomi Arayomi." *YouTube*, 4 Jan. 2021, www. youtube.com/watch?v=rCDFYw9bkDo.

3. Rumble. (n.d.). *Insider Exposes Freemasonry as World's Oldest Religion and Luciferian Plans for The New World Order* [Video]. Rumble. https://rumble.com/vhgzmp-insider-exposes-freemasonry-as-worlds-oldest-religion-and-luciferian-plans-.html

4. "Occupy With Apostle Tomi Arayomi and Apostle Jane Hamon." *YouTube*, 17 June 2022, www.youtube.com/watch?v=cTFaqhcqKfk.

5. *Discernment*. 14 Nov. 2023, dictionary.cambridge.org/us/dictionary/ english/discernment.

6. "The Great Reset Exposed | Babel Study Series Finale." *YouTube*, 29 Nov. 2020, www.youtube.com/watch?v=qfP3-k37VQ4.

7. *Why Covenants Are Powerful | Apostle Joshua Selman | by Matthew...* www.facebook.com/nkemchormatthew/videos/why-covenants-are-powerful-apostle-joshua-selman/348035880587022.

8. Prince D (2020) Applying the blood: How to release the Life and Power of Jesus' Sacrifice. Destiny Image Publishers, Inc., Shippensburg, PA

9. HISTORY. (2023, April 30). *The UnXplained: CURSE OF KING TUT KILLS 7 ARCHAEOLOGISTS (Season 5)* [Video]. YouTube. https://www.youtube.com/watch?v=1uF6O1KSW2E

10. Reporter, Guardian Staff. "Astroworld: Deaths of 10 People at Houston Concert Ruled Accidental." *The Guardian*, 20 Dec. 2021, www.theguardian.com/music/2021/dec/16/astroworld-festival-deaths-ruled-accidental.

11. Steinberg, Brooke. "Taylor Swift Fans Claim 'post-concert Amnesia' Due to Bizarre Phenomenon." *New York Post*, 30 May 2023, nypost.com/2023/05/30/taylor-swift-fans-claim-post-concert-amnesia-due-to-bizarre-phenomenon.

12. Congail, M. (2019, April 30). *BURNING MEN – The Myth of the "Wicker Man" in Celtic Europe*. Balkan Celts. https://balkancelts.wordpress.com/2013/10/05/the-wicker-man/

13. LiveNOW from FOX, Breaking News, Live Events. "Burning Man 2023: Death Under Investigation as Flooding Strands Thousands." *LiveNOW From FOX | Breaking News, Live Events*, 3 Sept. 2023, www.livenowfox.com/news/burning-man-festival-death-under-investigation-as-flooding-strands-thousands.

14. "Iniquity." *Merriam-Webster Dictionary*, www.merriam-webster.com/dictionary/iniquity.

15. "Pride." *Merriam-Webster Dictionary*, 12 Nov. 2023, www.merriam-webster.com/dictionary/pride.

16. Rap Zone. "Rappers Who Were Caught on Camera Selling Their Soul.. (Trippie Redd, Juice Wrld and MORE!)." *YouTube*, 12 Feb. 2023, www.youtube.com/watch?v=afi7tZbxEYQ.

17. OWN. "Beyoncé on Her Alter Ego, Sasha Fierce | the Oprah Winfrey Show | Oprah Winfrey Network." *YouTube*, 17 Aug. 2019, www.youtube.com/watch?v=4AA5G8vCl9w.

18. Foreman, Kelsie. "Who Are the Next Freemasons?" *Utah Business*, 5 Mar. 2020, www.utahbusiness.com/ freemasons-original-social-network.

19. Rumble. (n.d.). *Insider Exposes Freemasonry as World's Oldest Religion and Luciferian Plans for The New World Order* [Video]. Rumble. https://rumble.com/vhgzmp-insider-exposes-freemasonry-as-worlds-oldest-religion-and-luciferian-plans-.html

20. Lanum, Nikolas. "'Satanic Golden Medusa' Abortion Statue Outside New York City Courthouse Ruthlessly Mocked: 'Monstrosity.'" *Fox News*, 26 Jan. 2023, www.foxnews.com/media/ satanic-golden-medusa-abortion-statue-new-york-city-courthouse-ruthlessly-mocked-monstrosity.

21. LuKe10559. (2014, August 26). *John Ramirez-Ice Bucket Challenge-a voodoo ritual* [Video]. YouTube. https://www.youtube.com/ watch?v=LRP6r59_46Y

22. Arias, P. (2023, March 9). Dozens of Colombian girls hospitalized with 'anxiety' after playing with Ouija board. *Fox News.* https://www.foxnews.com/world/ dozens-colombian-girls-hospitalized-anxiety-playing-ouija-board

23. *Can Ouija Boards Trigger Demonic Possession?* (2015, August 7). Psychology Today. Retrieved November 7, 2023, from https://www.psychologytoday.com/us/blog/its-catching/201508/can-ouija-boards-trigger-demonic-possession

24. White, A., MD. (2012, January 5). *Abortion and the ancient practice of child sacrifice.* https://biblearchaeology.org/research/contempo-rary-issues/2243-abortion-and-the-ancient-practice-of-child-sacrifice

25. *What is Cymatics? Science of Visible Sound Explained.* (n.d.). Journey of Curiosity. https://journeyofcuriosity.net/pages/what-is-cymatics-how-to-explained

26. Nigel John Stanford. (2014, November 12). *CYMATICS: Science vs. Music–Nigel Stanford*

    [Video]. YouTube. https://www.youtube.com/watch?v=Q3oItpVa9fs

27. Emoto, Masaru. The Hidden Messages in Water. Atria Books, 2004.

28. *Before you continue to YouTube.* (n.d.). https://www.youtube.com/@KevinLAEwing

29. *MEA | Search Result.* (n.d.). Ministry of External Affairs, Government of India. https://www.mea.gov.in/search-result.htm?25096/Yoga:_su_origen,_historia_y_desarrollo#:~:tex-t=The%20word%20'Yoga'%20is%20derived,and%20body%2C%20Man%20%26%20Nature.

30. Groveonline. (2010, September 2). *The truth behind yoga.* Daniel Grove's Blog. https://groveonline.wordpress.com/2010/09/01/truth-behind-yoga/

31. *legion—Quick search results | Oxford English Dictionary*. (n.d.). https://www.oed.com/search/dictionary/?scope=Entries&q=legion

32. *What the Bible Says About Helel*. www.bibletools.org/index.cfm/fuse-action/topical.show/RTD/cgg/ID/20200/Helel.htm.

33. *What Is the Gap Theory? (The Ruin and Reconstruction Theory?)*. (n.d.). Blue Letter Bible. https://www.blueletterbible.org/faq/don_stewart/don_stewart_654.cfm

34. Quayle, Steven (2002) *Genesis 6 Giants*. End Time Thunder Publishers. Bozeman, MT.

35. "Cedar Tree Facts, Types, Identification, Diseases, Pictures." *Coniferous Forest*, www.coniferousforest.com/plants-trees/cedar.

36. *True Legends: Holocaust of Giants (Video 2017)—Plot—IMDB*. (n.d.). IMDb. https://www.imdb.com/title/tt7651072/plotsummary/

37. Drummond, J. (2023, July 26). *The Nephilim and the Sons of God—Biblical Archaeology Society*. Biblical Archaeology Society. https://www.biblicalarchaeology.org/daily/biblical-topics/hebrew-bible/the-nephilim-and-the-sons-of-god/

38. Knibb, M. (1974) *The Book Of Enoch*. Oxford University. https://scriptural-truth.com/images/BookOfEnoch.pdf

39. Patterson, S. (2020, May 25). *Let both grow together*. Let Both Grow Together. https://letbothgrowtogether.wordpress.com/blog/

40. Laura, C. &. (2014, September 23). *HEBREW WORD STUDY – SHOOTING THE ARROW*. Chaim Bentorah. https://www.chaimbentorah.com/2014/09/hebrew-word-study-shooting-arrow/

41. *Spirituality in America today.* (2022, March 10). A Study of Spirituality in America. https://spiritualitystudy.fetzer.org/blog/spirituality-america-today

42. Jones, B. J. M. (2023, September 29). In U.S., 47% identify as religious, 33% as spiritual. *Gallup.com.* https://news.gallup.com/poll/511133/identify-religious-spiritual.aspx#:~:text=WASH-INGTON%2C%20D.C.%20%2D%2D%20Nearly%20half,say%20they%20are%20neither%20religious

43. Barna Group. (2023, June 27). *Meet those who "Love Jesus but not the Church"–Barna Group.* https://www.barna.com/research/meet-love-jesus-not-church/

Printed in the USA
CPSIA information can be obtained
at www.ICGtesting.com
LVHW020353170624
783362LV00029B/928